A PICTORIAL HISTORY OF TEXAS

A PICTORIAL HISTORY OF TEXAS

BY HERBERT AND VIRGINIA GAMBRELL

E. P. DUTTON & CO., INC.
NEW YORK

First Edition

Library of Congress Catalog Card Number: 60-12109

Sources and Dates of Previously Copyright Illustrations

P. 17T, 17B, Bishop, Morris: *The Odyssey of Cabeza de Vaca,* © by The Century Co., 1933; p. 32TL, 36T, 40T, 53BR, 54B, Castañeda, Carlos E.: *Our Catholic Heritage in Texas, 1519-1936,* © by Von Boeckmann-Jones Co., 1936; p. 58B, DeShields, James T.: *Border Wars of Texas,* © by Mrs. Matt Bradley, 1940; p. 6TL, 12B, 55B, 77TR, Dobie, J. Frank: *Events in Texas History,* © by Republic National Bank and Trust Company, 1935; p. 16B, 34T, 35B, 36CR, 36C, 36BL, 36BR, 80, 106T, 109BL, 117T, 117B, 134C, 142T, 142BR, 162T, 162B, 163T, 163BR, 163BL, Fields, F. T.: *Texas Sketch Book,* © Humble Oil and Refining Co.; p. 108BR, Gambill, Birdie Brenholtz: *We Are Texas,* © by Banks Upshaw and Company, 1936; p. 19B, Garcilaso de la Vega: *The Florida of the Inca,* © by The University of Texas Press, 1951; p. 43TR, Heusinger, Edward W.: *Early Explorations and Mission Establishments in Texas,* © by The Naylor Co., 1936; p. 76TL, 159TR, Hogan, William Ransom: *The Texas Republic,* © by University of Oklahoma Press, 1946; p. 15T, 28TL, 31TR, Lea, Tom: *Calendar of Twelve Travelers Through the Pass of the North,* © by Tom Lea, 1946; p. 178, Lea, Tom: *The King Ranch,* Little, Brown and Company, © by King Ranch, 1957; p. 181BL, 181BR, Masterson, V. V.: *The Katy Railroad and the Last Frontier,* © by University of Oklahoma Press, 1952; p. 13TR, 13C, 13BR, *Natural History Magazine,* March 1937, © by The American Museum of Natural History; p. 82BL, 179T, Neville, A. W.: *The Red River Valley Then and Now,* © by North Texas Publishing Co., 1948; p. 8TL, 8BL, 10TL, 10C, 10BR, 11T, 26TR, *A Picture Book Introduction to the San Jacinto Museum of History,* © by San Jacinto Museum of History Association, 1950; p. 32BR, Priestley, Herbert Ingram: *The Coming of the White Man, 1492-1848,* The Macmillan Company, © 1957 by Bessie B. Priestley; p. 130B, Red, William Stuart: *A History of the Presbyterian Church in Texas,* © by The Steck Company, 1936; p. 72TL, 123BL, Reid, Mary: "Fashions of the Republic of Texas," © *Southwestern Historical Quarterly,* 1942; p. 2BL, 2BC, 3TR, 21B, Skelton, R. A.: *Decorative Printed Maps of the 15th to 18th Centuries,* © by Staples Press Limited, 1952; p. 210-11, State Board of Control: *State of Texas Building,* © by The Steck Company, 1937; p. 115T, © by *The Texas Bankers Record,* February, 1960; p. 193B, Webb, Walter Prescott: *The Great Plains,* Ginn and Company, © by Walter Prescott Webb, 1931; p. 20T, 28-29C, Wharton, Clarence: *The Lone Star State,* © by The Southern Publishing Company, 1932; p. 73B, Writers Program: *Texas, A Guide to the Lone Star State,* Hastings House, © by Texas State Highway Commission, 1940.

CONTENTS

A PICTORIAL HISTORY OF TEXAS

CHAPTER 1

CHESSBOARD

Alvar Nuñez Cabeza de Vaca, Spanish nobleman, shivered, naked and emaciated, on the cold sands of Galveston Island on a windy November day in 1528. Around him lay half-dead bodies of his companions and wreckage of a makeshift boat that had miraculously brought them from Florida. Somewhere in the water was his royal commission. The greatest monarch in Europe—Charles, King of Spain and Holy Roman Emperor—had sent him to America to protect the royal interest. He was treasurer of the grand expedition led by Pánfilo de Narváez to add all North America to the Spanish Empire; de Vaca was to inventory its fabulous wealth.

That was last year.

If Narváez had only listened to de Vaca last year, or even last week; but Narváez never listened to anybody. No subordinate, no woman, could tell him what to do. He would conquer this gold-rich land of the Fountain of Youth that had twice defeated Ponce de León and claimed his life. He would find riches greater than rebellious Cortes had struck in Mexico. He would do it in his own imperious way.

On Good Friday, 1528, undaunted by dissensions, desertions, and shipwreck on the way, Narváez had anchored in Tampa Bay, 400 men and wives of several officers with him, banners flying, and a learned harangue ready to be read to the natives, who were nowhere to be seen.

To the empty huts of a deserted village he read his manuscript which explained how this land now belonged to His Catholic Majesty and the natives were his subjects. Next day the Indians returned, unwilling to accept the New Order which they neither had heard nor could have understood. Narváez knew there was plenty of gold *mas allá* and he ordered officers and their wives, soldiers and colonists, friars and horses ashore to search it out, inland. The ships would await them farther along the coast.

De Vaca warned him to stay near his transports. The women rebelled and refused to land—a sybil had foretold many of the troubles already experienced and had promised catastrophe in the interior. Sure that their husbands were lost forever, they consoled themselves with new mates

Columbus arrived in the West Indies in 1492 and claimed the whole unknown hemisphere for Spain. Santo Domingo, Cuba, Jamaica and other islands were quickly overrun and they became springboards to the continent which many thought and hoped was Asia. From Cuba came the men who found what it was.

OF EMPIRE

among the crew as the ships cruised nearly a year before returning to Cuba.

On through "great lakes, dense mountains, immense deserts, and solitudes" Narváez and his men marched, finding a few poor Indians—all hostile—and no gold. Lost, living on palm shoots, their bony horses spavined and galled, they stumbled eventually back to the coast; but ships and wives they never found. They were destitute and stranded, their banners tattered, their armor tarnished.

Pánuco (Tampico) was the nearest Spanish outpost, no one knew how many leagues away. Death stalked the overland route, death by starvation and by arrow. Not a man among them knew how to build or sail a boat, but in desperation they put together five crude, unseaworthy scows, without "tools, nor iron, nor forge, nor tow, nor resin, nor rigging." Iron things were hammered into nails and axes. One by one they killed the skinny, useless horses—one every third day—to eat the flesh and cover the boats with the hides—except the leg skins that made water bottles. Horse tails and manes were plaited into rope. In gratitude and irony they called the place the Bay of the Horses (*Bahía de Caballos*).

Indians killed ten men as they worked, forty more died of starvation and disease, but at last 242 miserable, spiritless men crowded into five flimsy skiffs, hoisted sails that had once been shirts, and started westward. The gunwales were only nine inches above water; any movement might sink the boats.

Narváez, irascible to the end, still shouted orders and still disregarded de Vaca's advice until, in exasperation, he announced it was every man for himself. Off the coast of Texas one midnight, as Narváez sat in his boat, "the north wind blowing strongly took her unobserved to sea, and they never knew more of their commander."

Now, on the Texas island he called Ill-Fate (Malhado), de Vaca, his men too feeble to stand or even swat insects, was confronted with a hundred Indian warriors "who if they were not large, our fears made giants of them." He knew what red-bearded, one-eyed Narváez had done to Indians in Florida when his men were able to fight; but now among this starved remnant of that once formidable command "it would have been difficult to find six that could rise from the ground."

To the Spaniards' astonishment, these Texas Indians warmed them and fed them and, moved by their "suffering and melancholy destitution, sat down among us and . . . lament[ed] so earnestly that they might have been heard at a distance." Then they literally carried the helpless strangers to their huts to nurse them back to health.

Thus the first sojourners from Europe bedded down in Texas.

Hundreds of miles to the south of them other Spaniards had bedded down in a land of incredible riches.

Nine years earlier, in 1519, Hernando Cortes—ruthless, proud, devout, romantic, and practical as only a medieval Spaniard could be—blundered into the land of the Aztecs. Governor Velásquez of newly conquered Cuba had appointed him to explore and report, expecting to reap all honors and profit of everything Cortes should find, for he was *adelantado* of all he had discovered or "might hereafter discover." Cortes was to be his faithful agent, not to conquer or colonize, but only to examine and report to Velásquez. Or so Velásquez thought.

In February, 1519, Cortes assembled at Santiago, Cuba, 617 soldiers and seamen, plenty of arms and munitions, and—most important of all—sixteen magnificent horses, more valuable than any sixteen men or sixteen guns for the work ahead. Velásquez, too late, suspected Cortes' motives and loyalty and revoked his commission; but Cortes defied him and sailed off with his men and guns and horses. Off Yucatán he picked up a castaway Spaniard, Aguilar, who could speak Mayan. Then at Tabasco he defeated an Indian army "that filled the plain" but was no match for Spanish cavalrymen, guns, and horses—which in their ignorance the Indians believed to be a single gigantic, irresistible demon.

For his great exploring expedition Governor Velásquez naturally chose his companion, Hernan Cortes. They had conquered Cuba together and they knew each other well—too well to trust each other completely. On second thought, the Governor canceled the commission but could not prevent Cortes and his men from sailing.

The defeated chief gave Cortes twenty maidens, among them "a truly great chiefteness," captive daughter of an Aztec noble. Cortes renamed her Doña Marina and made her his mistress and translator. As Cortes gave orders, Aguilar repeated them in Mayan, then Marina spoke them in Aztec. No other explorer had such a communication device.

Now Cortes set out on a course that would make him a timeless hero—or a forgotten rebel. Without a shadow of legal authority, he dared to act in the name of the King, and as His Majesty's self-appointed agent took formal possession of this great and limitless land, which he renamed New Spain.

After Mass on Palm Sunday, Cortes admonished the Tobasco Indians to forsake their false gods and sailed to Veracruz Harbor. Here he learned of Montezuma and his fabulous realm. This was not the old familiar routine of Indians trying to be rid of white men by telling them the gold was *mas allá*. Messengers from Montezuma himself brought bales of finely woven fabrics and magnificent golden ornaments set with gems; hesitant and apprehensive, they asked these strangers whence and for what they had come. Were they servants of the White God, or gods themselves? Cortes did not say but promised to visit the Aztec ruler and sent him presents, including a gilded helmet he wanted filled with gold dust. To his amazement, the helmet came back full of gold and with it more and richer and finer gifts, intricate featherwork and cartwheels of solid gold and silver. But one thing was lacking—there was no invitation to come inland.

Here was a land richer than any Spaniard had dreamed of, rich with precious things easily transported, peopled by men skilled in arts and crafts, governed by an emperor who was afraid of his uninvited visitors. The earthly paradise that Columbus was always about to find, that Ponce de León and countless others died seeking, lay before him. It was his for the taking.

Legally he was a rebel, outlawed by Governor

All the island governors were eager to find the mainland, whether it be Asia or a new world, and to add new lands to their domains. Governor Garay of Jamaica, an enterprising, imaginative empire builder, sent Pineda to find the coast line and select a site for Garay's future colonies. His expedition had no connection with Cortes', which set out from Cuba about the same time. Pineda began his explorations on the Florida peninsula, gradually following the coast line to Veracruz, where he and Cortes surprised each other. He stopped in Texas on the way home.

Velásquez. If he returned to Cuba, he would be disgraced, probably executed, and the riches of the Aztecs would be Velásquez's. Worse still, he had already committed lese majesty when he claimed all this land for the King, a king that did not know him or where he or this land was. If he returned to Spain empty-handed, he would pay the penalty for his impious gasconade—and while he awaited punishment someone else would snatch the prize now within his grasp.

Cortes was a soldier, not a lawyer, but he recalled enough law to know that a Spanish municipality was directly under the King. If his men organized themselves into a town under the King's protection and the town council elected him to take charge, he would have a legal leg to stand on—at least until he could conquer Montezuma and all his lands and people and receive from his grateful sovereign appropriate honors, emoluments, and titles.

In June the Villa Rica de la Vera Cruz was created and Cortes, its captain general and *adelantado,* wrote the King that all that had been done was for His Majesty's glory and the spread

Pineda's voyage lasted nine months; it was the most careful examination of any part of the North American coast that any European had made. It demonstrated that there was no water route to China from the Caribbean and that the land was probably a continent that geographers knew nothing about. With great accuracy, in spite of the crudity of his instruments, he made a serviceable map of the region he visited. This map served Governor Garay when he came to the mainland himself. It was the first map of the Texas coast and is still preserved in Spain.

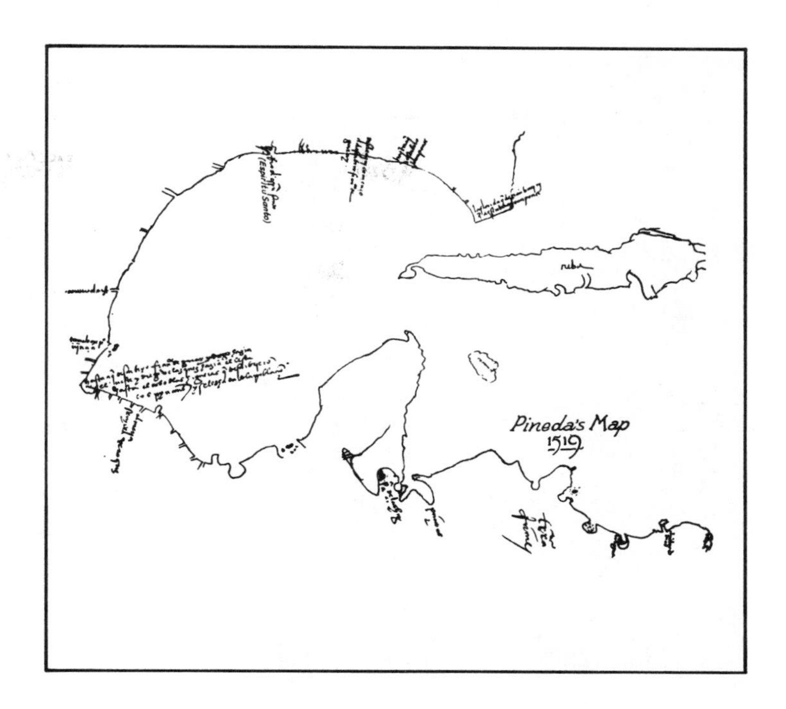

of the Gospel. Then he scuttled his ships, mutilated or hanged those who questioned his course, and prepared to meet this mighty Montezuma and take from him all that he possessed.

Before he could march to greet the monarch who only wished he would go away, four Spanish ships sent by another governor hove in sight. Cortes hurried to the beach and arrested a notary and two soldiers who were busy ceremonially claiming possession for Governor Garay of Jamaica. These vessels, commanded by Alonso Alvarez de Pineda, had traced the Gulf coast from Florida to Veracruz, seeking a water route to the spice lands. Pineda mapped it as he went and claimed it all for Garay. When he saw Cortes detain his men as trespassers, he turned his ships back to the Rio Grande. At the tip end of Texas, while he tarried forty days for ship repairs, he dutifully claimed that land for Garay, there being no Cortes there to interfere. Then he took his map—the first one ever made of the Texas coast—to Garay, who planned other expeditions from Jamaica to Texas.

But Cortes—and Fate—reserved Texas for other Spaniards.

At the end of August, 1519, Cortes was ready to visit Montezuma, convinced that "there is everything in this country which existed in that from which Solomon is said to have brought the gold for the temple." Hadn't a *cacique* told him so?

"Montezuma," the Indian said, "is lord of many kings; his equal is not known in the world; in his house many lords serve barefooted with eyes cast down to the ground; he has thirty thousand vassals in his empire each of whom has one hundred thousand fighting men; each year twenty thousand persons are regularly sacrificed in his dominions—some years fifty thousand. Montezuma dwells in the most beautiful, the largest, and the strongest city in the world—a city built in the water, possessing a noble palace and plaza, one the center of an immense traffic. Hither flock princes from all the earth bringing incalculable riches. No lord however great is there who does not pay tribute, and no one so poor is there who does not give at least the blood of his arm."

Under the spell of this vision of a feudal empire vaster and richer than any that ever existed, Cortes with 400 Spaniards began the tortuous, hazardous ascent to Tenochtitlan, 7,000 feet higher and many leagues inland. He picked up aid from Montezuma's restive vassals and aided by a shrewdness that seemed to the Indians almost supernatural, avoided the numerous traps and pitfalls. Lush country they traversed, and populous; not so rich as he expected, but hope fed on hope.

Tenochtitlan, Montezuma's capital, stood on an island in briny Lake Tezcoco, a mile and a quarter above sea level. Three broad cement viaducts connected it with the mainland, and an aqueduct brought water to its closely packed inhabitants, whose number was variously estimated from 70,000 to 200,000. It was built around a huge central plaza which was surrounded by a nine-foot wall decorated with carved serpents. Here the "immense traffic" Cortes had heard of was daily conducted, and the causeways and streets teemed with traders and artisans, priests and Aztec officials. The whole city was dominated by the awesome, gigantic pyramid sacred to Huitzilopochtli, the war god, and Tezcatlipoca, god-of-the-breath-of-life. It was 300 feet wide at bottom. At its apex, 150 feet above ground, priests offered human sacrifices to propitiate the principal deities. To the unsensitive nose of a Spanish cavalryman these holy men "stink like sulphur and have another bad smell like carrion."

On October 15, 1519, Cortes ended his six weeks' march at the south causeway of Montezuma's dazzling capital. There the master of things-as-they-were reluctantly met the embodiment of things-to-be. Each, after the custom of his people, extended formal greetings: Montezuma kissing the ground and offering Cortes roses; Cortes placing his own necklace around the Aztec's neck and embracing him.

Montezuma lodged his Spanish guests in his own palace, taking humbler quarters for himself. Convinced that the white men were representatives of the White God who had promised to return and evict anyone who ruled Tenochtitlan, Montezuma did not resist but instead agreed to become Cortes' mouthpiece. Stored gold and gems were divided among the conquerors, after the King's fifth had been scrupulously set aside. Cortes stopped human sacrifice, smashed idols, and had Mass sung atop the great pyramid. He embraced Montezuma as his brother and taught him to play cards and other Christian pastimes while his men discreetly searched for treasure. It was too pleasant to last.

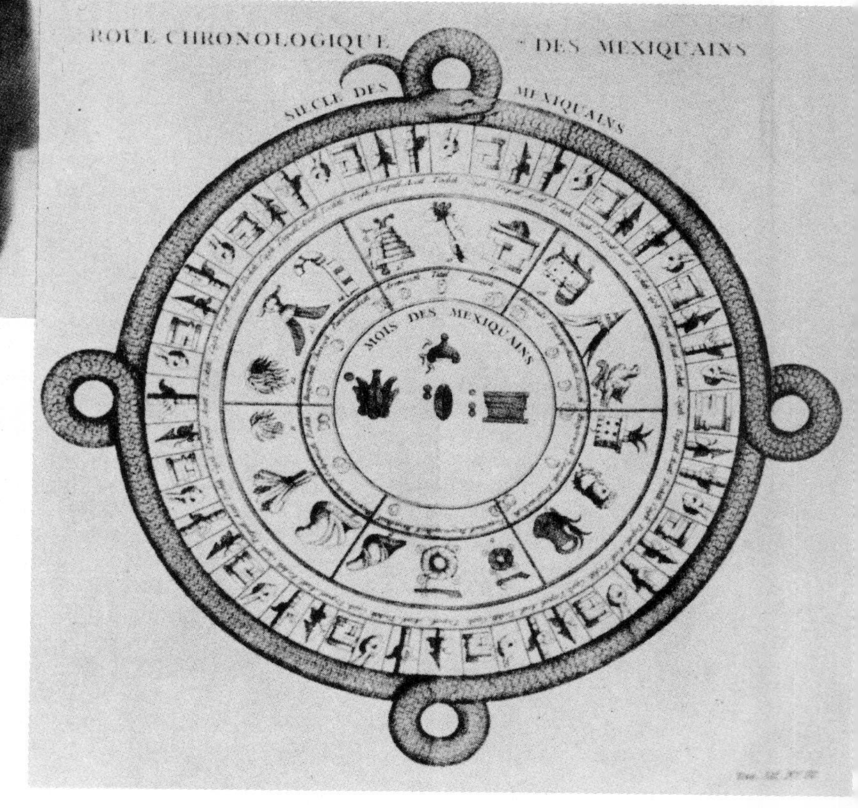

The gods of Mexican Indians were more numerous than the dialects, and representations of them created many art forms. When Indians accepted the new and powerful God of the conqueror, they did not abandon their old deities. Like other primitive people, they studied the stars and from astronomy they devised remarkably accurate calendars. This Mayan calendar shows a year of 18 months, 360 days. The Aztecs had a similar calendar before the Spaniards came.

The Aztecs had developed many crafts. Their textiles were particularly fine, woven of cotton or maguey fiber, and bearing intricate patterns. The uppper classes wore robes of brilliant colors. Some of their fabrics were decorated with representations of the sun, of local or tribal gods, or geometric designs. They also made paper on which they recorded scenes, such as this one, which depicts the administration of justice.

"This palace belongs to you," Montezuma told Cortes, then confessed that Mexico was property of Quetzalcoatl, the white god, not the Aztecs. He surrendered it all to Cortes, recognized him as the god's agent, and promised to carry out the orders that Cortes gave for his master across the sea.

Brave, foolhardy Pedro de Alvarado ended the entente cordiale *by ordering a massacre of the Aztecs while Cortes was thwarting Narváez on the coast. After Cortes dashed back into Tenochtitlan with 1,000 Spaniards, Montezuma was killed and uncounted thousands of Aztecs were mowed down, but the white men were evicted, losing all their guns, much treasure, and 450 men. That was* la noche triste, *June 30, 1520. But Cortes still had his indomitable will and his interpreters. He chastized and conciliated Indians, built barges, and in May besieged the capital. Until August 13, 1521, slaughter, destruction, and famine did their work. The Indians now knew that Cortes was neither god nor priest; but they also knew he was master of Mexico.*

As vividly as any Spanish chronicler's story of the conquest of Mexico, these pictures by native Aztec artists tell the Indian's version of the epic. The Aztecs, who had no alphabet, had for centuries recorded the great events in their history in pictures. None are more graphic and moving than these depicting the sudden, catastrophic end of their empire. Despite their unfamiliarity with some things they drew—bearded men, European animals, weapons, and (until too late) the rules of civilized warfare—these pictures are accurate enough to serve as illustrations for Cortes' own official reports of these stupendous events.

Spaniards land at Veracruz with cows, sheep, pigs, horses. Doña Marina tells a startled native what to do.

In the final attack on Tenochtitlan, the Spaniards used gunboats on the lake to raze landing places for cavalry.

"With this event," the inscription reads, "the Mexicans were finished." Cortes and Doña Marina (seated) are receiving the vanquished Cuauhtemoc, the last Aztec emperor, with the honors of war. He was an admirable leader who won the grudging respect of his conquerors even while refusing, under torture, to tell where treasure was hidden. A magnificent monument to Cuauhtemoc stands in Mexico City. Montezuma has none.

Into Veracruz came 15 ships and 900 men from Cuba. They were under the command of Pánfilo de Narváez, a powerful and loyal man who carried with him orders to arrest Cortes as a rebel against Governor Velásquez. But Cortes knew the land and he knew Spaniards; he slipped out of the capital with half his men, found and overpowered Narváez's sentries, then seized Narváez and forced a surrender. Narváez lost an eye and his liberty; his men willingly joined Cortes to revel in the halls of Montezuma; and New Spain was never to be Velásquez's.

When Cortes returned with his new followers to Tenochtitlan, a desperate battle was in progress there. By July 30, 450 Spaniards and innumerable Indians lay dead, and all white men were evicted from the city. But the Aztecs were demoralized, Montezuma was dead, and Cortes could not give up. Almost by a miracle he was able to retake the city in mid-August, 1521; he retook the site, but all was in ruins except a fragment, which Cortes ordered pulled down, so that a Christian city could be built there to the glory of the true God and His Most Catholic Majesty.

From the new City of Mexico radiated exploring parties, finding few mines but many unworked mineral lodes toward the northwest. Promptly agencies of Spanish government were set up and agents of the King took the power Cortes expected to be his. The crown was generous to the man who claimed to have given it "more kingdoms than your ancestors left you cities"; generous in titles, lands, and allotments of Indians, generous in everything but what Cortes coveted: power.

His conquest of Mexico meant that after 1521 the southern half of the continent would be Spanish, and that for three hundred years Mexico City would be the center of Spanish authority, where a viceroy ruled in a palace of royal splendor.

Signature of Pánfilo de Narváez.

CHAPTER 2

Alvar Nuñez Cabeza de Vaca

THE LAND IN BETWEEN

Into this viceregal capital of the kingdom of New Spain, built in a decade on the ruins of Aztec Tenochtitlan, came in the year 1536 Alvar Nuñez Cabeza de Vaca with a tale to stir imagination and whet avarice. Since his shipwreck on the Texas coast in 1528, he had lived naked among Indians, sometimes as guest, more often as slave, occasionally as medicine man, always as a careful observer, always a loyal servant of the King who sent him to this bewildering new world.

Still hardly able to bear the weight of a shirt on his weather-toughened back, he recounted to Viceroy Mendoza the Narváez fiasco and, more importantly, his seven-year odyssey in Texas. The Viceroy listened avidly.

The "large and well-formed" island Indians who saved him from death made the Spaniards "physicians, without examination or inquiring for diplomas," after pestilence had killed half the tribe and many of the Spaniards. They answered de Vaca's demurrer by shutting off his food until he agreed. He practiced a strange blend of Christian

prayer and witch doctoring, but it worked. "Our method," de Vaca said, "was to bless the sick, breathing upon them and recite a Paternoster and an Ave Maria, praying with all earnestness to God our Lord that He would give them health. . . . In His clemency He willed that all . . . should tell the others that they were sound and in health, directly after we made the sign of the blessed cross over them."

He and his companions dug roots with bleeding fingers; traded shells and beads for skins and ochre and tassels of deer hair on the mainland, always returning faithfully to their island masters. As death reduced the number of Spaniards from eighty to four, hunger sometimes drove them to eat the dried flesh of their dead, to the horror of the Indians who were keeping alive on ant eggs, spiders, worms, and rattlesnakes. When the four Spaniards escaped to the mainland, they were made captives of different tribes and thus separated, but eventually were united with a friendlier tribe that made all of them medicine men. They brought back one Indian from the dead; extracted an arrow from the shoulder of another, and performed other feats that the medical faculty of Salamanca had never achieved. They were saved

from starvation by eating green prickly pears and the scraps they scraped from animal skins. Two dogs kept them alive several days.

When at last de Vaca and his companions reached the Rio Grande near El Paso del Norte, they pronounced it as wide as the Guadalquivir. Their fame as medicine men made their journey a triumphal march. These Indians had food, conducted them to the next tribe, introduced them as children of the sun who could heal or destroy, "and other lies."

"They bade them conduct us with great respect to where people were numerous; and that wheresoever they arrive with us, they should rob and pillage the people of what they have, since this was customary."

On the way they picked up a copper bell with a face carved on it, and five arrows tipped with

The King gave Alvar Núñez's ancestor the name Cabeza de Vaca in the 13th century for directing his army through a secret mountain pass marked by a cow's skull. This sketch of Cabeza de Vaca's arms made by an enemy erroneously shows two cows' heads.

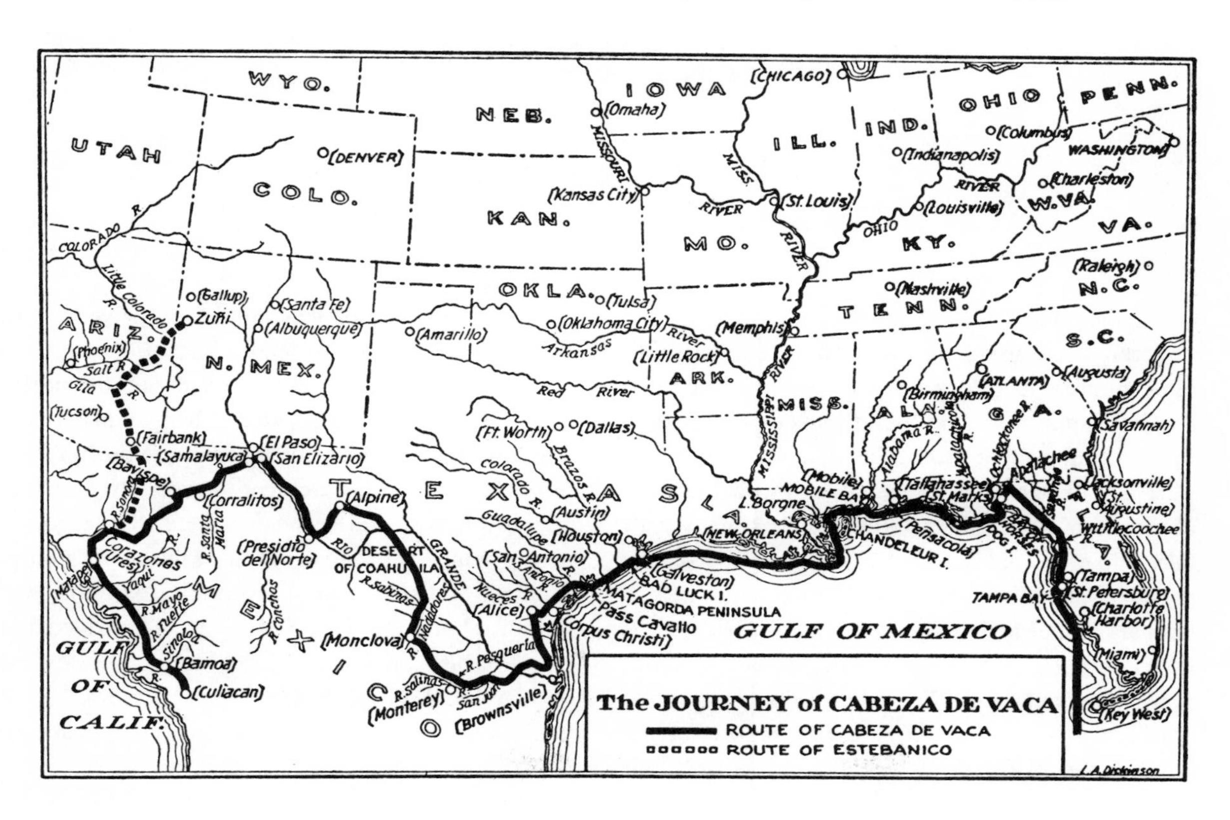

PLVS VLTRA

La relacion que dio Aluar nu-
ñez cabeça de vaca de lo acaeſcido enlas Indias
enla armada donde yua por gouernador Pã-
philo de narbaez / deſde el año de veynte
y ſiete haſta el año d treynta y ſeys
que boluio a Seuilla con tres
de ſu compañia.:.

Cabeza de Vaca's Relación *(1542), first book about Texas.*

emeralds, and heard innumerable rumors of mineral-rich country *mas allá,* of great cities with large houses. De Vaca himself saw none of them but in the mountains he found signs of "gold, antimony, iron, copper, and other metals."

It was this hint of great cities, more than the chronicle of heroism, that gave value to de Vaca's tale, when he told it to the Viceroy in the palace in Mexico City in July, 1536. Why shouldn't there be "another Mexico" to the north? There was fabulous Peru, now being exploited, to the south. It was the Viceroy's official duty to penetrate "the northern mystery," to verify Indian reports of the Seven Cities of Cibola, where the streets were full of the workshops of goldsmiths and silversmiths.

De Vaca declined to lead an expedition for the Viceroy; he wanted to explore and rule the northern region, but he wanted the King himself, not a subordinate in Mexico, to commission him. He left Estebanico, his black companion, to guide the Viceroy's men, and sailed for Spain. He reported to the King, petitioned for an *adelantado's* commission, and sat down to write the first book ever written about the Texas country. He arrived too late for his commission, and had to be content with a bootless mission in South America. The noblest of the gentlemen adventurers appears no more in the Texas story.

The royal commission de Vaca wanted and deserved went to a man to whom the King could not say no: Hernando de Soto. A Knight of Santiago, a hero of the conquest of Peru and a gentleman from whom Charles V borrowed money, De Soto was the equal of Cortes in audacity, tenacity, and resourcefulness, and vastly superior to the other *conquistadores*. His services to the crown entitled him to whatever he asked, and he asked for Florida, that vague, vast, enigmatic land where Ponce de León and Narváez had found neither gold nor the Fountain of Youth. De Soto knew that he could find there "another Peru," richer than Mexico; equally certain were hundreds of noble Spaniards who sold their possessions to share in the enterprise. So many volunteered that De Soto had to select the 600 he could take by examining their muscles and the set of their jaws, as well as their pedigrees.

Before July 1, 1539, they were at Tampa Bay, among Indians who remembered Narváez and were no more hospitable to this new invader. A few pearls he found, but no evidence of gold. But beds of pearls, lodes of gold and silver and maybe emeralds must be in this vast region where white men had never settled; De Soto willed it to be so, and his men assumed it true.

Relentlessly, unfalteringly his men marched through Florida, Georgia, the Carolinas, Tennessee, Alabama, Mississippi, Arkansas, Oklahoma,

Hernando de Soto.

Hernando de Soto, who, "with nothing more than blade and buckler," had helped conquer Peru, proposed to conquer and pacify the North American mainland. With 600 gallant men, he landed at Tampa Bay in May, 1539, trekked through southeastern United States, discovered the Mississippi River in 1541, and a year later died and was buried in its waters. Luis de Moscoso led remnants of the expedition into Texas and finally to Mexico. Probably the "most remarkable exploring expedition in the history of North America," its endurance and heroism and dedicated leadership became legendary.

Louisiana. It was the most systematic, detailed exploration that any Spaniards had made in the New World. They found rich agricultural lands, navigable rivers, industrious Indians—every resource except what they sought. There was no flaw in De Soto's leadership, nothing wrong with his technique, no dissension among his followers. It was simply that the land itself defeated him; it refused to yield what it never had. There just weren't any precious metals.

Unaccustomed to having his will thwarted, De Soto refused to believe the obvious, and on and on his men searched. He discovered the Mississippi River in May, 1541, which was enough to make him immortal; but that was not what he sought. He outwitted and outmaneuvered Indians in a hundred battles, but that gave him no elation—he had done it all before in Central America and in Peru. He had managed, against odds, to keep most of his men alive; but that was no more than a knightly "gentleman by all four descents" was bound in conscience to do.

By his standards he had failed, and for that there was no extenuation. Could his pride bear the thought of returning empty-handed? Or living to hear that another man had found in Florida that which had eluded him? Ill, as much from broken will as from disease, he called his men about him, named Luis de Moscoso to lead them, received extreme unction, and died on May 21, 1542, near his great river and was buried in its bed.

Moscoso was no hero; he preferred a gay life among Christians to exploring and gold hunting; his goal was "to get out of the land of Florida in the shortest time." First he tried the land route to Mexico, through Texas as far as the Brazos River. He no longer sought gold, only a route to white settlements. He heard of buffalo but did not see them, or anything else that pleased him. He never knew that he was within a day's march of another, less bedraggled band of Spaniards when he called a halt, returned to the Mississippi, and built boats that brought 311 dispirited men to Pánuco (Tampico) on September 11, 1543. Texas they had seen, and Texas had nothing that any of them wanted to see again. For them there was nothing between the Rio Grande and the Atlantic to excite cupidity or merit Spanish exertion.

Meantime destiny beckoned other Spaniards toward the Pacific and through western Texas. Spanish legend and Indian folklore agreed that north of Mexico was the Strait of Anian which led to China, and the Amazon islands, and the Seven Cities of Cibola, and other wonders and rich provinces. What de Vaca reported as Indian rumor in 1536 was soon accepted as true.

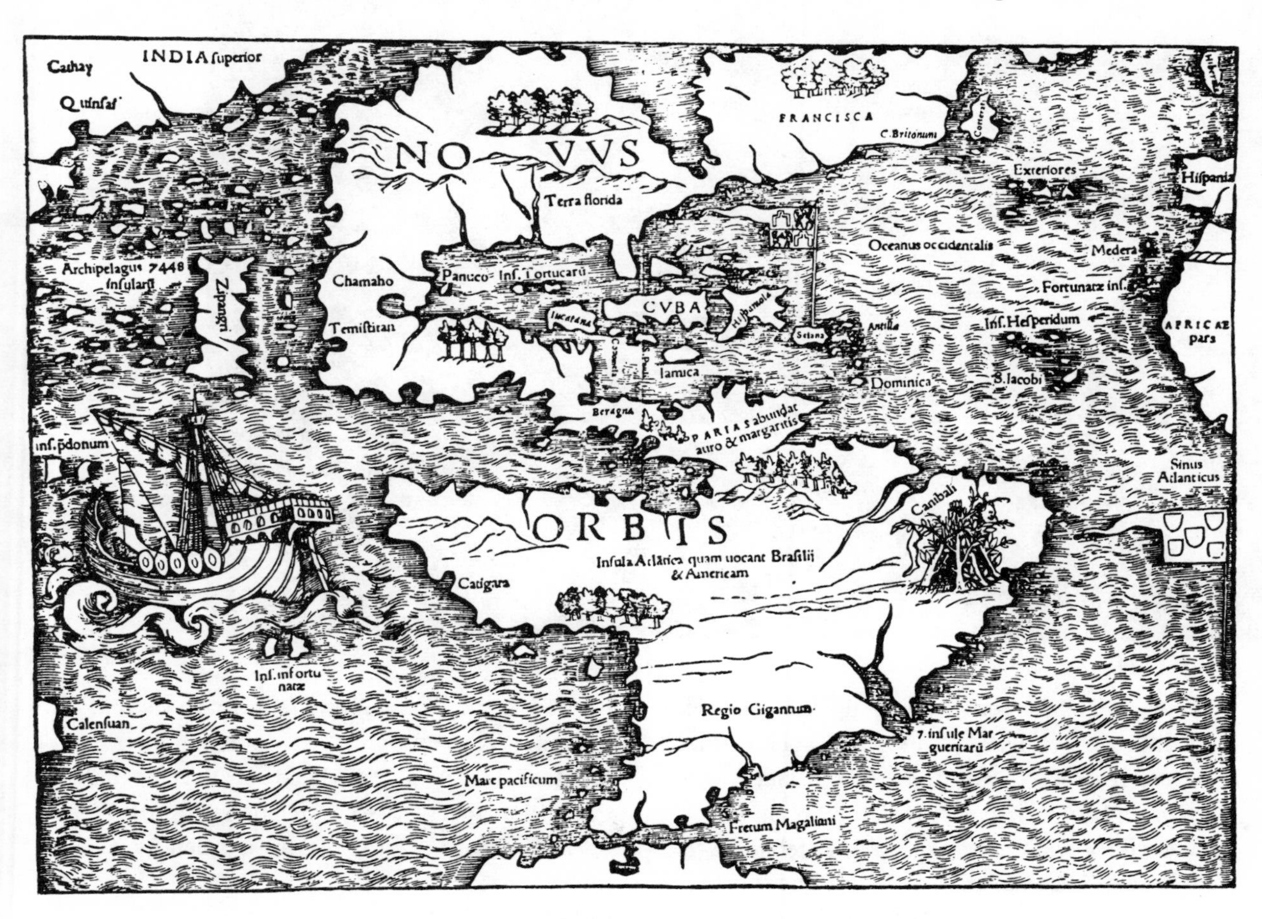

The shape of the Americas as Europeans imagined it soon after the voyages of discovery. This woodcut was published in a new edition of Ptolemy's Geographia *edited by Sebastian Münster (Basle, 1540).*

Antonio de Mendoza, setting up the first viceregal court in Mexico, fell under the spell of these tales and resolved to add these fabled lands to his domain and to christianize their inhabitants.

When de Vaca hurried to Spain, Estebanico, his black man, became an oracle on the northern mystery and the guide to lead Fray Marcos to the Seven Cities, which Estebanico had never seen. The friar thought he saw one city from a distance, hurried back "with more fear than victuals" to tell the Viceroy, and was chosen to ride as spiritual leader at the head of the magnificent expedition that was to take possession of Cibola.

In February, 1540, the most splendid expedition yet assembled in Mexico started from Compostela toward the Seven Cities: 300 soldiers, 700 Indian allies, 1,000 extra horses and a walking commissary of cows, sheep, and pigs, with supply ships following along the Gulf of California. Francisco Vásquez de Coronado, dashing young governor of New Galicia whose wife was the richest heiress in Mexico, led the procession in gold-plated armor and gold helmet. He was confident of himself and his men, and that Fray Marcos, who rode beside him, knew the way; he had been there.

They deployed east, west, north; found new lands, friendly and hostile Indians, made maps, kept diaries. Then, where New Mexico, Arizona, and Mexico meet, they found Cibola! When the men saw it, one of them noted, "such were the curses that some hurled at Friar Marcos that I pray God to protect him from them. It is a little, crowded village, looking as if it had been crumpled all together."

That was the first of the Seven Cities, and the others were no better. It was the beginning of a disillusionment that only increased during the next two years. The men discovered the Colorado River of the West, the Grand Canyon, and buffalo, and other natural wonders; but no gold, no silver, no pearls or emeralds, not even any Amazons.

This coat of mail, worn by a Spanish soldier of the 17th century, is made of caribou horns linked with brass rings.

In winter camp near Albuquerque, dispirited but still determined, they listened to an Indian they called the Turk. He was, he said, from Gran Quivira, a land greater and richer than anything white men had seen. Its ruler was lulled to sleep by golden bells hung in apple trees; its rivers were broad and deep and the fish bigger than horses; and common utensils were of pure gold. This must be what they sought; Quivira, not the Seven Cities. Not Mexico, not Peru could compare with their vision of it.

Coronado's gun? This was found near Odessa in West Texas. It is of 16th-century design, probably Dutch, and may have been lost in the sand by one of Coronado's soldiers in the 1540's.

Early picture of the humpback cattle or buffalo. Cabeza de Vaca was the first European to describe these improbable animals he encountered in Texas. Coronado's men told more about them: "There was not one of the horses that did not take flight when he saw them first, for they have a narrow, short face, the brow two palms across from eye to eye, the eyes sticking out at the side, so that, when they are running, they can see who is following them." Buffalo roamed Texas until the 1870's.

In the spring of 1541 Coronado moved his men eastward into Texas. In the Panhandle they marveled at the endless, treeless plains where "when a man sits down, the horizon surrounds him all around at the distance of a musket shot" and the feet of thousands of men and horses and cattle "leave no more trace where they have passed than if nothing had been there—nothing—so that it was necessary to make piles of bones and cow dung now and then so that our rear guards could follow the army." It was a land to swallow up strangers.

As they traveled across Texas, they found little food and less water. With 36 men Coronado pressed on to Quivira, relying more on directions from the Indians they encountered than on the Turk, who seemed increasingly bewildered. When they reached central Kansas "where there was no gold nor silver nor any trace of either," the Turk confessed that his job was to lose the Spaniards on the plains, not to find Quivira, which did not exist. For this the white men, of course, executed him; then found their way back to New Mexico and finally, quarreling among themselves, to Mexico. Another land had defeated Spanish courage and rapacity. Another explorer reported there was nothing in Texas that Spaniards needed.

For a hundred years it was so.

Francisco Vásquez de Coronado came to Mexico at age twenty-five with the first viceroy. Five years later he commanded the grandest exploring expedition ever assembled on the continent and for two years chased the chimera. After he returned empty-handed, he lived for twenty-five years the humdrum life of a Mexico City councilman.

But there were men in Mexico who had something they wanted to give, not take from, the red men in Texas. They were Franciscan missionaries who were pushing northward from Mexico City, telling Indians of the true God and teaching them the arts of civilization. They established a mission, San Juan Bautista, on the Rio Grande and were ready to expand into Texas. But the royal treasury paid the cost of missionary work, and officials were more willing to christianize rich Indians than poor ones, like the Texans.

In New Mexico, Indians lived in villages or *pueblos;* they were more easily civilized and might have undisclosed wealth. For this and other reasons New Mexico was more attractive than Texas. In 1598 Juan de Oñate led a small army of soldiers and settlers there and conquered it; but the settlements did not flourish. Santa Fe was founded in 1609 and around it missions multiplied. Sixty thousand Indians were converted in a generation, and the Spaniards and the christianized Indians and the unconverted Indians lived peaceably together.

At the end of the century the land west of Texas was securely Spanish.

The friar, armed only with breviary and psalter, was as great a conquistador as the man in armor. Souls were as important as gold—and more plentiful.

Proof that God, as well as the King, loved the Indians came in 1531 when the Virgin Mary appeared to a peon at Guadalupe.

PSALTERIVM,
Anphonarium Sanctorale, cũ
Psalmis, & Hymnis, positis in
suis locis proprijs vniuscuiusq̃,
diei festi totiusanni, nũc primo
cum licentia excusum.

MEXICI.
Excudebat Petrus Ocharte.
M. D. LXXXIIII.

The Franciscans realized that while they were converting Indians they were also making history, and they took pains to record and publish it. This handsome volume, dedicated to the reigning Spanish king, was printed in Valladolid in 1611. Note the symbolic figures.

QVARTA·PARTE
de la Chronica General de Nro. Padre, San Francisco y su Apostolica Orden, Compuesta por Fray Antonio Daça yndigno frayle Menor diffinidor de la Santa Prouincia de la Concepcion, y Chronista General de su Orden
Al Rey Nuestro Señor Don Philipe III
Año De 1611
S. Antonio de Padua
S. Juan de Capistrano
Impresa en San Francisco de Valladolid por Juan Godines de Millis, y Diego de Cordoua

Juan de Oñate was an American-born conquistador; his wife a descendant of Montezuma. In May, 1598, he led 400 men and 130 families through El Paso del Norte to colonize New Mexico. They brought 7,000 head of stock and 83 wagons loaded with tools and implements. The conquest of New Mexico followed quickly. The gentle Pueblo Indians willingly listened to the friars, wilder Indians were quelled by the soldiers, and Oñate explored east and west. In 1608 Oñate lost the governorship, but the next year Santa Fe was founded and for the next seventy years the western prong of New Spain was securely Spanish.

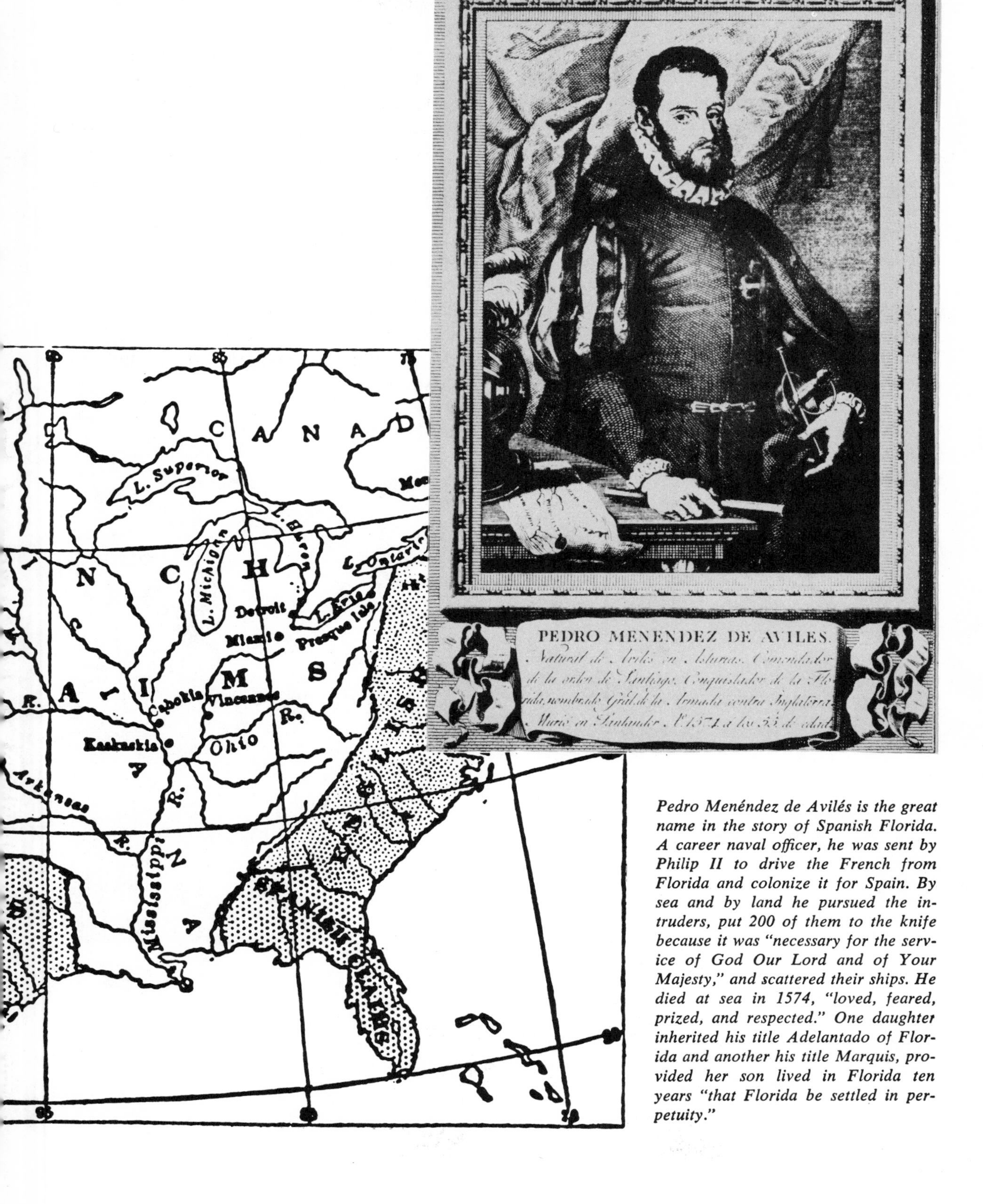

Pedro Menéndez de Avilés is the great name in the story of Spanish Florida. A career naval officer, he was sent by Philip II to drive the French from Florida and colonize it for Spain. By sea and by land he pursued the intruders, put 200 of them to the knife because it was "necessary for the service of God Our Lord and of Your Majesty," and scattered their ships. He died at sea in 1574, "loved, feared, prized, and respected." One daughter inherited his title Adelantado of Florida and another his title Marquis, provided her son lived in Florida ten years "that Florida be settled in perpetuity."

But to the east of Texas a challenge to Spain's monopoly appeared. Spanish "Florida"—which stretched from the Rio Grande through all the eastern half of North America—had been partly explored but not colonized. Neither Catholic France nor Protestant England believed that God willed that all the gold and land and peoples of the New World should be Spain's exclusively; and they claimed their share—which meant as much as they could take.

France acted first. In 1562 she began sending Huguenots who claimed Florida for her and built a fort at the tip of the peninsula to menace Spanish treasure fleets. Spain sent ships, soldiers, colonists, and missionaries under her greatest sea fighter, Menéndez de Avilés, to plant her standard firmly. He hanged intruders "not as Frenchmen but as Lutherans," founded St. Augustine (1585), scattered forts along the Atlantic, and built Jesuit missions. The French were evicted, but neither Spanish settlements nor Spanish missions flourished. Still no gold; still no Castilians willing to labor like peasants; still few Indians willing to receive the gospel and the arts the priests offered.

At least it was a Spanish land, not merely by papal grant, but by occupancy—defensive occupancy. France never came back, but English sea dogs such as Hawkins and Drake occasionally harassed the coast; still Spain retained her tenuous hold on eastern North America.

At the end of the century Spain held Florida; Spain held New Mexico and Spain idly claimed—by default rather than conquest—Texas, the Land in Between.

Signature of Coronado.

CHAPTER 3

THE CROSS AND THE SWORD

From 1536 to 1685 Texas was a sort of No-Man's Land, its oblivious, contented Indians undisturbed by agents of civilization. Occasionally little bands of Spaniards from New Mexico wandered into western, sometimes central, Texas, and others forayed north of the Rio Grande; but they found no reason to remain. The Mexican viceroy ordered no settlement in Texas; neither his king nor any other ruler wanted that land. For a century and a half everyone was content to leave Texas and her Indians alone.

It was the Atlantic coast of North America that attracted Europeans, and there England and France were getting footholds. England planted her little colonies in regions Spain claimed but never occupied; and France, evicted from Florida, began building her American empire to the north —far from any Spanish stronghold.

France found the St. Lawrence River (1534), then the Great Lakes, and finally the Mississippi that De Soto had discovered for Spain a century earlier. Like Spaniards, the French searched for a strait to Asia, which nobody ever found, and for gold and silver, which did not exist in that region either. But they found fur aplenty, which made them rich. If it wasn't gold it was the next best thing to send to Europe. Soldiers, trappers, traders, missionaries streamed from France to the north of America, gradually driving a wedge southward to separate Spanish New Mexico from Spanish Florida.

Texas slept at the bottom of that wedge.

La V. M. Maria de Jesus de Agreda. Predicanda
á los Chichimecos del Nuebo mexico.

The Lady in Blue whose apparition in Texas Indians saw is identified as a Spanish nun.

Various groups of Texas Indians were seeing miraculous apparitions of the Lady in Blue who told them to beg for Spaniards to teach them her religion. Missionaries in New Mexico interpreted this as a divine order; but the Viceroy did not. Friars also pointed out that some of these Indians were wealthy, bartering gold dust to foreigners who used it to make war on Spain. That, too, availed nothing. Spain was too weak, too beset by enemies, to seek Texas gold or save Texan souls until the 1680s, when this Land in Between suddenly became precious.

To Madrid came rumors of foreign intrigue. Diego de Peñalosa, who had left the governorship of New Mexico in disgrace in 1664, was at work in Paris. Calling himself the Count of Santa Fe (in honor of the capital from which he was banished), he was offering to lead the French to the Texas coast and to immensely rich provinces inland. Unexpectedly the pious prayers and petitions of a century were now answered: Spain began seriously to contemplate Texas. But she wavered indecisively and fatally, and suddenly her control over New Mexico broke.

This 1680 rebellion of the Pueblos was the most serious Indian challenge Spain had faced. These New Mexican Indians killed or drove out all white men and most christianized red men. The lucky ones fled to El Paso, where there was a mission, and established Ysleta Village nearby. New Mexico was lost to Spain for eighteen years, but one remote corner of Texas was securely Spanish.

Process of conversion explained (1579). Friars bring the Church to the Indians (center). *Creation, catechism, and the sacraments—even care of the sick—are illustrated for the instruction of the red men.*

Painting of La Purisima Concepción, believed to have been painted in Spain and stolen from a mission during the Pueblo Revolt of 1680. Two centuries later some Texans defeated a band of Comanches and found the canvas under one of their saddles. The Indians apparently used it for many purposes—none of them religious—while they had possession of it, and it was too badly damaged to be returned to the Church. The Franciscans and other orders gave many New World missions the name La Purisima Concepción in honor of the Virgin Mary.

After the Pueblo Revolt of 1680, Christianized Indians fled from various sections of New Mexico to El Paso del Norte, so named by Juan de Oñate on his way to take the region for Spain a century earlier. Near El Paso the Franciscans in 1682 founded a mission to minister to the refugees as well as to the nearby Tiguex Indians. The mission was first called San Antonio de la Isleta but the name was changed many times before Corpus Christi de la Isleta was chosen. Through the years it was commonly referred to as the Isleta mission, while the town that grew up nearby is always referred to as Ysleta. This village, founded by refugee Indians a generation before San Antonio, is the oldest continuously inhabited place in Texas, and had a population of 1,600 in 1950.

Three French ships bearing La Salle's 400 colonists skirted the Texas coast in January–February, 1685, seeking a good harbor.

On the coast of Texas came an even more ominous threat. Robert Cavelier, Sieur de La Salle, American viceroy for Louis XIV, landed a party of French men and women at Matagorda Bay in February, 1685, without the opposition—or even the knowledge—of any Spaniard. He built a fort and a stockade—a base for vast operations.

La Salle, that morose, haughty empire builder, had served his king well in Canada. He had discovered Niagara Falls, sailed the Great Lakes, then explored the Mississippi to its mouth. There he inscribed a column: "Louis the Great, King of France and Navarre, reigns, April 9, 1682." He visualized this limitless valley as the center of a vast New France that would expand east and west, overriding Spanish claims and evicting Spaniards—and Englishmen, and any others in his way. He hurried home to share his dream with his king at Versailles.

Louis XIV personally interviewed La Salle and

commissioned him to govern a region extending from Canada through Texas into mine-rich northern Mexico. With 400 ill-assorted companions—inexperienced soldiers, gentlemen, families, girls wanting husbands, and alleged artisans—he left France on July 24, 1684.

En route La Salle and Beaujeau, his fleet commander, quarreled; Spaniards captured one of the ships; La Salle became ill. In January, 1685, the expedition sailed past the Mississippi and continued westward to Texas. On February 15 they landed in Matagorda Bay. In the course of the landing, one ship was wrecked, supplies sunk or stolen by Indians who killed guards, captured colonists, and lurked about menacingly—to the French colonists their first days in Texas seemed an omen of worse things ahead. To top it off, Beaujeau defiantly sailed back to France, taking with him cannon intended for the fort.

About two hundred discouraged men and a few women—including soldiers who did not know how to use guns and artisans "no better," priests, friars, several children, and only a few men of frontier fortitude—established Fort St. Louis. It was an impressive name for what was no more than a makeshift French outpost; a timber and rawhide "fort" with eight cannon, surrounded by flimsy barracks, dormitories, and a corn patch. But at least there was fresh food—birds, prairie game, fish, turtles, and oysters—and a stout stockade to keep out Indians and Spaniards.

As the cold and hot months passed, La Salle and his colonists grew progressively irritable. When he took long, fruitless treks—first toward the mines of Mexico, then toward the Mississippi—colonists quarreled with one another, and disease and Indian arrows took a heavy toll. By Christmas, 1686, only 45 were left to attend midnight Mass.

On January 12, 1687, after drinking the King's health in cold water, for there was no wine, La Salle made a sort of farewell address to his shivering, hopeless colonists, then set off with ten armed men and two priests to find the Great River.

La Salle landed in Matagorda Bay, and his troubles began. The Amiable *and her cargo were lost in landing; the* Joli *sailed off with munitions; then the* Belle *sank. His colony was stranded.*

In Fort St. Louis, built of flotsam and logs, the French settled down for a long stay. The women learned to make edible the strange animals, birds, and reptiles the men brought in; the priests fitted up a chapel; and the other men, when not exploring, planted a garden and dressed pelts. None of them had ever seen such flora and fauna as they found in Texas.

He needed to get help from Canada before death took the frayed remnant of his colony.

A priest, two friars, a surgeon, and a few soldiers remained at Fort St. Louis with the women and children "to await the issues of the journey and the possible arrival of a tardy succor." It was a long and bootless wait.

Hampered by swollen streams, La Salle moved slowly eastward across the Colorado and Brazos rivers, his men quarreling over the division of food and other things, and plotting mutiny. La Salle's close-mouthed, stubborn arrogance only increased the dissension. When, on March 19, he went to bring back a laggard hunting party, he saw buzzards circling above the bodies of three of his men, murdered by their companions. As La Salle approached he was ambushed and shot through the head.

The murderers stripped his body, then "killed each other at various times for various reasons." La Salle's surviving companions pressed on to Canada, thence to France.

The Murther of Mons.r de la Salle

M. Vander Gucht Scul:

So remote was Texas in space and in interest, that Fort St. Louis had been there six months before any Spanish official heard of it; and then the news came not from Texas but from a French sailor who knew only that the French settlement was somewhere between Florida and Tampico. It took five years and nine expeditions to find it. Several times Spaniards were within a few miles of the place they sought; but the land was swampy and they decided sane people would not settle there.

As sailors scoured the coast, land expeditions from northern Mexico and New Mexico trekked into Texas. After two fruitless entradas, Governor Alonso de León of Coahuila captured an elderly Frenchman who was ruling a band of Indians like a king, sitting naked on a throne of buffalo hide. However, he was not one of La Salle's men. It turned out he had wandered into Texas from the North, and had lost not only his clothes but his mind. Whatever his Indian bailiwick was called, it obviously was not Fort St. Louis. He swore he could lead the Spaniards to La Salle's fort, but "in all his testimony the said Frenchman always lied," Father Massanet sadly records. Five parties by sea and three by land learned a lot of geography but found no French fort.

Then, on April 22, 1689, the fourth land expedition under Alonso de León came upon Fort St. Louis, silent and deserted. The men found "six houses, not very large . . . another larger house where pigs were fattened, and a wooden fort made from the hulk of a wrecked vessel. And, Father Massanet adds, "we found two unburied bodies, which I interred, setting up a cross over the grave. There were many torn-up books, and many dead pigs." No Frenchmen.

Starvation, desertion, epidemic, and an Indian raid had done the Spaniards' work for them. A few days later León found Jean L'Archeveque, who had been with La Salle's murderers, and Jacques Grollet, one of his sailors. They had missed the massacre at Fort St. Louis; from them he learned of La Salle's death and all the misfortunes that had plagued his colony from the day the Frenchmen arrived in Texas.

"Sir, I do not know what sort of people you are . . . We are French . . . We know well that you are Spaniards . . . we are sorely grieved to be among the beasts like these who believe neither in God nor in anything if you are willing to take us away you have only to send a message as we have but little or nothing to do. . . . Your very humble and very obedient Servant, Jean l'Archeveque de Bayonne." One of La Salle's men wrote this in red ochre on the back of the parchment on which this ship is drawn, and his companion wrote a message on the left margin. At first glance a priest thought it signed by the Archbishop of Bayonne! León's men found the Frenchmen "naked except for an antelope's skin, with their faces, breasts, and arms painted like Indians." At Mexico City the Viceroy gave them proper clothing and shipped them to Spain.

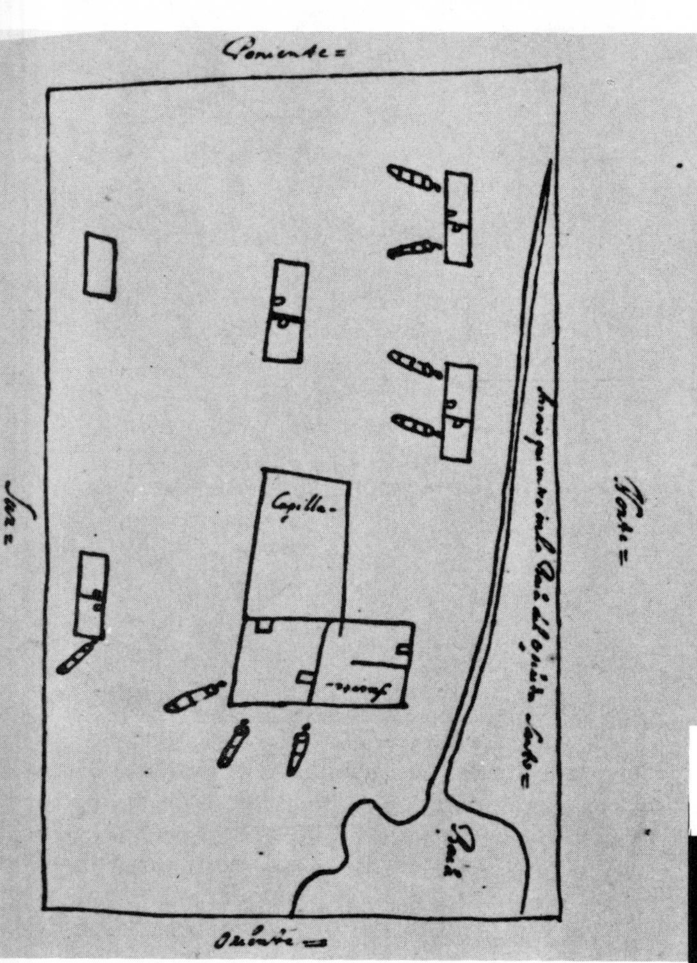

NAL ECH

1684 =

VSQVE
AD
168

Governor León caused full reports of the finding of Fort St. Louis to be written for the Viceroy and with them he sent drawings made on the spot showing the arrangement of the buildings and the eight cannon within the stockade. The chapel was the central as well as the largest building. The scribe also carefully copied the inscription he found beneath the cross at the principal entrance: "1684 Until 168_" No Frenchman survived to write the final date, and the Indians who killed them could not write. León sent beams from the fort to a church in Monclova.

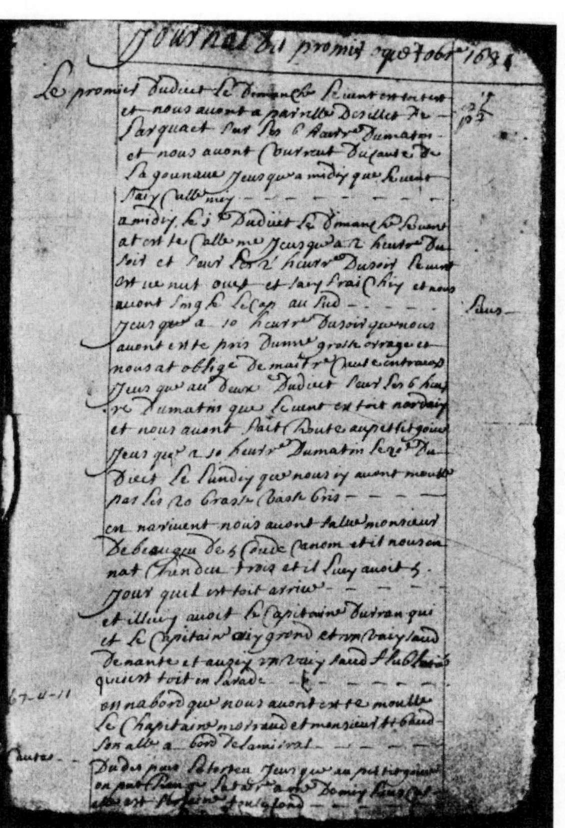

Page of the log of the Belle *as she neared Haiti October 1, 1684. The handwriting is fair; spelling could hardly be worse.*

This French venture was not much of a threat to Spain, but it made Spain Texas conscious. The Viceroy hurriedly decided to civilize and christianize the Texans. To that end León was appointed governor.

Father Massanet, who accompanied León, found the Tejas tribe providentially prepared to receive the Gospel. The chief knew of a Supreme Being; he pointed skyward at the word God; he carried a portable altar with Christian symbols and kept a light burning on it night and day. The Lady in Blue had visited his ancestors and he begged missionaries for his people. And that was more important to the friar than all the French forts in the world. Governor León, not ordinarily given to exaggeration, wrote the Viceroy that the Tejas were as civilized as the Aztecs and one of his captains, not to be outdone, declared León a second Cortes.

Still in a mood of action, the Viceroy ordered missionary work to begin in Texas July 5, 1689. Spain and France were at war again, which made control of Texas important; but the conquest was to be spiritual, not military.

In March, 1690, Father Massanet and four other priests, escorted by Governor León and 110 men with droves of cattle and stock and a bounteous commissary, set out from Monclova to the Tejas country. They paused near the coast for Massanet to set fire to what was left of Fort St. Louis "and in half an hour the fort was in ashes." As they neared the camp of the Tejas chief, they found two French boys and took them along. The chief met them at the Trinity River and conducted them to his house and fed them on boiled beans, *atole, pinole,* and *tamales,* "all very cleanly."

Corpus Christi Day "was celebrated with all solemnity and a procession, all the officers and soldiers, the Indian governor, and many of his people accompanying the procession and witnessing high Mass. Mass having been completed, the ceremony was enacted of raising the flag in the name of His Majesty (whom God protect) and I, the said General Alonso de León . . . accepted the obedience which they rendered to His Majesty, and in his royal name promised to befriend and aid them. I delivered to the governor a staff with a cross . . . giving him to understand . . . that which he should observe and do . . . that he should make all his families attend Christian teaching. . . . He accepted the staff with much pleasure, promising to do all that was required of him, and the company fired three salutes. Likewise . . . Fray Damian Massanet was given possession that he might instruct them in the mysteries of our holy Catholic faith." Thus San Francisco de los Tejas, the first Texas mission, was officially established near the Louisiana border.

In five days a chapel and house for the friars were built "in the midst of the principal settlement of the Texas." Another procession, another high Mass, another ceremony of investiture, and another distribution of presents; then all but three soldiers and three friars returned to Mexico with León and Massanet to report the King's standard firmly planted among the Texans. A brother, a nephew, and a cousin of the chief went along to tell the Viceroy how happy this made the Texans. Massanet reported, not to the Viceroy but to a friend, that there had been almost daily fights and stabbings among the soldiers, and that the lay brother who was in charge of first-aid found tepid wine "an excellent cure for stabs in the head."

The work began hopefully but, for the Indians, the novelty soon wore off. They would not move into the mission enclosure, and for all their professed desire to be taught, they were impudent and indifferent to Spanish manners and the road to heaven. Strange misfortunes befell them: floods, droughts, famine, diseases that killed horses and men—for all of which their medicine man blamed the padres. To win Texas for Spain against the forces of nature and human perversity was more than three friars and three soldiers could reasonably be expected to do.

By October, 1693, the Texan friars and the Viceroy's counselors, a thousand miles apart and studying different data, decided to give Texas back to the Indians. The friars, fearing massacre, buried their altar vessels, burned their log mission, and crept away between suns, not knowing that orders had been issued from Mexico instructing them to do so. They might be willing martyrs; but of tedium and frustration they had had enough.

Texas again belonged to its Indians at the end of 1693. Both France and Spain had raised their standards there; both had failed. Spain was willing to forget Texas—if France would. And the Indians were willing to be left alone.

Intricately wrought Spanish soldier's metal stirrup.

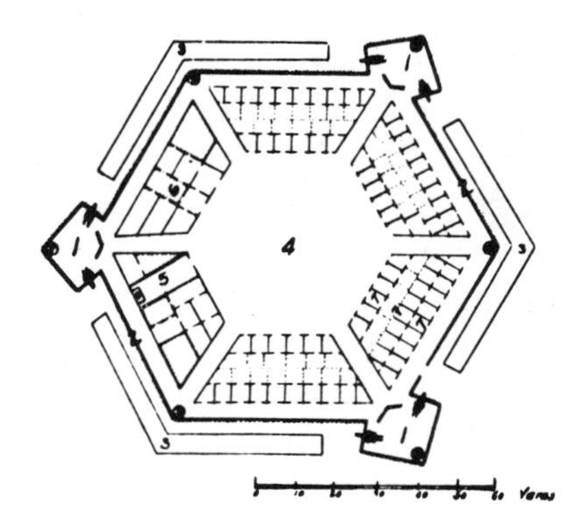

1. Bastions. 2. Palisades. 3. Ditches. 4. Plaza. 5. Church. 6. Stores and commandant's quarters. 7. Barracks for the officers.

Plan of Presidio de los Adaes

Spain's vigor was declining everywhere; but France was still building her American empire. Biloxi (1699) and Mobile (1702) she planted to harass Spain in the Gulf; then Natchitoches (1713) and New Orleans (1718) to hold the Mississippi Valley and expand into Mexico.

French plans included Texas. From French outposts scouts and traders were making friends of the Tejanos, learning their languages, supplying them arms and goods. Cadillac, governor of French Louisiana, who was instructed "to open trade with the Spaniards in Mexico," received in 1713 a puzzling letter from Spanish Fray Francisco Hidalgo who, twenty years before, had worked among the Tejas. He wanted French help to convert these Indians.

Governor Cadillac promptly sent Louis Juchereau de St. Denis, a dashing, cunning young frontiersman, to find Father Hidalgo, trade goods for grain and stock, and generally spy out the land. St. Denis, who had been in Texas a time or two before, visited the Tejas—who nicknamed him Big Legs—then proceeded toward the Rio Grande, trading and observing and looking for Hidalgo.

Late in 1714 St. Denis presented his compliments to astonished Captain Diego Ramón, commander of San Juan Bautista on the Rio Grande. Ramón arrested him for trespassing, then hospitably made him a house guest. As St. Denis waited to know what punishment the Viceroy would assess him, he charmed everyone at the presidio, especially Ramón's granddaughter, Doña Maria, who promised to marry him. He was sent a prisoner to be grilled by the Viceroy, who might have condemned him to death. But so adroit was St. Denis that he returned to Texas as second-in-command of the expedition to keep out the French! He paused at San Juan long enough to marry Doña Maria and enjoy a brief honeymoon, then guided the Spaniards to the Tejas country.

Twelve friars, six families, supplies for farms, missions and a presidio (fort), and a thousand head of stock moved into Texas along with twenty-five soldiers commanded by St. Denis' new cousin-in-law in April, 1716. A little east of the site of San Francisco de los Tejas they built San Francisco de los Neches for Father Hidalgo; then they set up five missions in the Nacogdoches–San Augustine–Robeline area, and a presidio. At each the commander distributed tobacco, trinkets, and clothing, and told the Indians that God and the Spanish king loved them—better than any Frenchman.

The Tejanos had "an undiminished capacity for receiving gifts" but their desire for the intangibles the friars offered had not increased, and French traders made them economically independent. Three of the missions moved to San Antonio after fifteen years of failure; the others languished until 1771, the friars comforting themselves by remembering that "the gospel does not command us to convert, but only to preach."

After 1718 the area around San Antonio was a center of Spanish activity. First came the mission San Antonio de Valero and the presidio of Béxar; by 1731 missions San José (finest architecturally), Concepción (sturdiest), Espada, and Capistrano were in operation along the river.

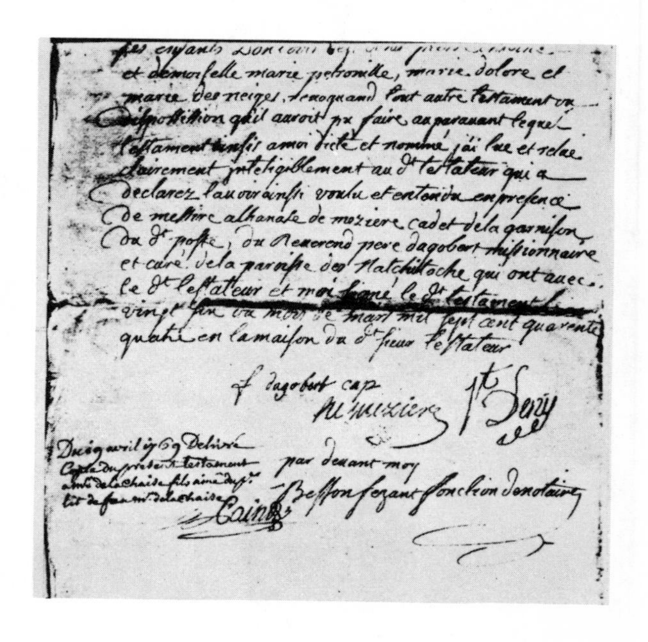
ses enfants [illegible]
et demoiselle marie petronille, marie dolore et
marie des neiges, revoquand tout autre testament ou
disposition qu'il auroit pu faire auparavant lequel
testament ainsi a moi dicte et nommé j'ai lue et relue
clairement intelligiblement au dt testateur qui a
declarez l'avoir ainsi voulu et entendu en presence
de messire athanase de meziere cadet de la garnison
du dt poste, du Reverend pere dagobert missionnaire
et curé de la paroisse des Natchitoche qui ont avec
le dt testateur et moi signé le dt testament le
vingt six du mois de mars mil sept cent quarante
quatre en la maison du dt sieur testateur

f dagobert cap
deMeziere
St Denis

Du 6 avril 1769 Délivré
Copie du present testament
[illegible] de la Chaise fils ainé du s.
[illegible] de feu m. de la Chaise
[illegible]

par devant moy
Besson fezant fonction de notaire

Last will of Louis Juchereau de St. Denis, glamorous frontiersman of 18th century Texas.

Año De 1735

Desde Cuio año Tubieron Principio los Casamientos por la Vª. Aunque se Fundò este Pueblo el Año de 1731 por el mes de Março.

1 Joseph Flores Nacion Patumaco, Con Efioenia nacion Pajalat.

2 Juachin Antonio nacion Patumaco, Con Brigida nacion Pachalaque.

3 Christoval grande nacion Patalca. Con Ba[illegible] nacion

Nuestra Señora de la Purisima Concepción de Acuña operated near San Antonio 1731–94. Franciscans brought neophytes from an east Texas mission to construct this chapel that still stands and is occasionally used. Some of its frescoes are still visible and its register of births, deaths, and baptisms has been preserved. It has marvelously withstood time.

There are many legends about the "rose" window of San José mission, most famous remnant of Spanish architecture in Texas.

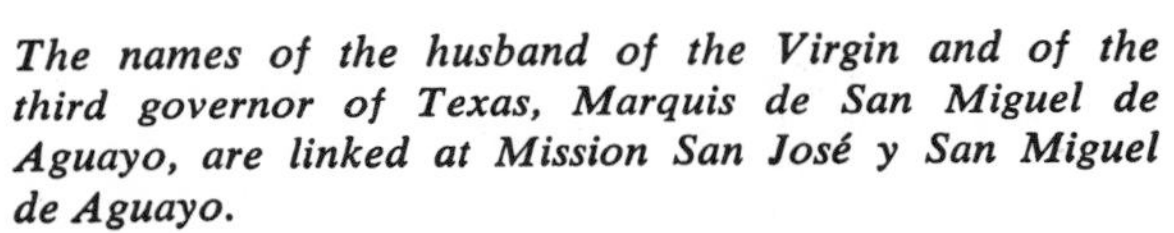

The names of the husband of the Virgin and of the third governor of Texas, Marquis de San Miguel de Aguayo, are linked at Mission San José y San Miguel de Aguayo.

San José was the second of the San Antonio missions, founded 1720. Its chapel is probably the finest erected in New Spain. Its single tower with open belfry is reached by spiral stairs of twenty-three hewn oak logs. The high wall surrounds chapel, friary, refectory, dormitories, shops, and granaries, all of stone. A canal brought water from the river through the enclosure thence to the surrounding fields. Before its secularization in 1794 it was the most successful of all the Texas missions. It was painstakingly restored in 1949.

San Francisco de la Espada Mission

In 1731 fifteen families of Canary Islanders—52 persons—arrived footsore and weary, to start the town originally called San Fernando. Spanish missionaries, Spanish soldiers, Spanish villagers—San Antonio was now indelibly Spanish.

The missions were walled villages in which the Indians lived while the friars taught them religion, crafts, and manners. The chapel was the finest structure in the enclosure, but there were many others: dormitories, workrooms, storerooms, granaries, mills, smithies, tanneries, textile factories—everything a self-sufficient community needed. Each mission had acres and acres of farm and grazing land.

It was actually a sort of vocational reform school with a week-long Sunday school added. Only when they escaped to the woods were mission Indians out of sight of their teachers. One friar wrote:

"It is necessary that the missionary take them out to the fields . . . that he go about with them in planting and harvesting, and that he take care that they guard the stock. He must count them, go with them . . . accompany them in all their occupations. . . . Every day it is necessary to give rations to each Indian, for if the food is left where they can get it, in two days the whole supply is consumed."

When not working or eating, Indians attended religious services and heard expositions of Christianity "with similes and arguments adapted to their inexpressible stupidity." The friars gave varied vocational training "both because it is their duty and because it is the most important means of subsistence"; and when Indians feigned illness to escape work and get special food, the friars "pretend to be deceived" to keep their charges happy.

It was a hard life for Indians and friars alike, and the results were meager. There were 1,700 Indians in Texas missions in 1740; about five hundred forty-five years later; none in 1821. The

San Juan Mission

buildings were in ruins and the friars gone; Texas had been neither converted nor civilized, but the missions made good Spain's claim to the province.

There were towns, too—Spanish-type towns, where tillers of soil and herders of cattle lived, and commuted to the country. First was San Antonio, founded by royal decree in 1722 with a chart of its streets and plazas, but its first families did not arrive until 1731 to lay out the streets, build San Fernando Church, and later a palace for the governor. Its *ayuntamiento* of nine men included four who could write their own names.

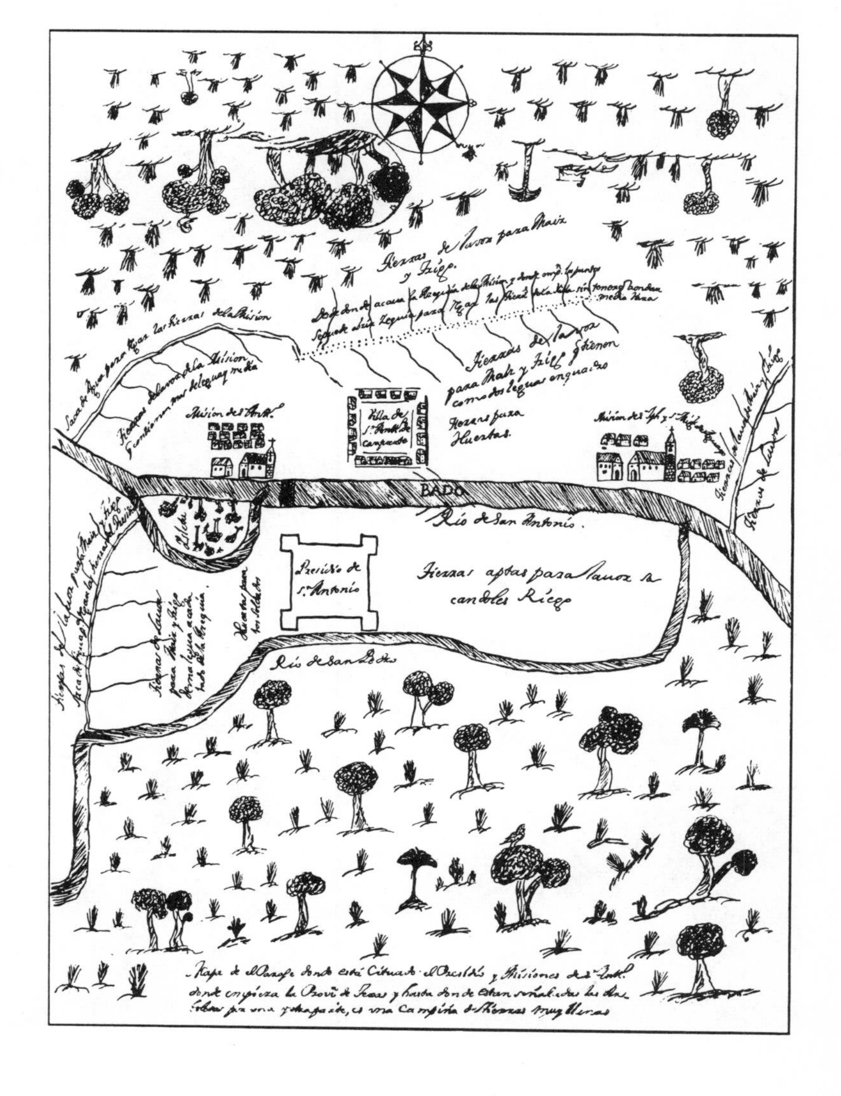

Spanish power in Texas centered at San Antonio after 1718. That year Father Olivares brought interpreters, tools, sheep, oats, and chapel fittings from the Rio Grande to found the mission San Antonio de Valero (the Alamo), which operated until 1793. Nearby the Presidio San Antonio de Béxar was established as the military center of Spanish Texas. Then in 1731 came the Villa San Fernando de Béxar, after years of planning. Settlers came from the Canary Islands to become the First Families of Texas. Above. *The town was laid out in Spain, and its location in relation to the river and the missions is shown on Aguayo's map of 1730.*

Near the Louisiana border was Nacogdoches, a town created without anybody's permission. After Spain got Louisiana from France (1762), she moved all the missionaries and soldiers and settlers from East Texas to San Antonio. This suited the friars and soldiers, but the 500 civilians protested so loudly that, when granted permission to move a few miles eastward, they went back to their own land in East Texas and built the Stone Fort around which grew the town of Nacogdoches. This was unauthorized but it was winked at. La Bahía, a straggling village on the Guadalupe River near the coast, had sprung up near a presidio. The place is now called Goliad.

Only in San Antonio, capital of Texas after 1773, was there urban social life. Perhaps 3,000 civilians of European blood lived in Texas at the end of the Spanish period. Twenty-seven missions had been dedicated and ten presidios established, but an official sorrowfully recorded in 1819 that Texas was inhabited principally by "barbarians and wild beasts." Nevertheless, Spain indelibly marked the land; she had managed to keep it from France and to retain her feeble hold.

La Bahía del Espíritu Santo.

Provinª de los Texas. } { Jurisdiccion de Bexar.

Estado que Manifiesta el Numero de Vasallos, y Havitantes que tiene el Rey en esta Jurisdiccion con distincion de Clazes, Estados, y castas de todas las Personas de ambos Sexos, inclusos los Parbulos

Nombres de las Poblaciones	Omb.s	Mug.s	Niños	Niñas	Esclabos	Esclabas
Presidio de Sn Antonio de Bexar y Villa de Sn Ferndo	231	239	269	216	4	7
Mision de Sn Jose	41	31	26	25		
Ydem de Sn Juan Capistrano	53	26	13	7		
Ydem de Sn Francisco de la Espada	32	28	30	6		
Ydem de Nra Sra de la Concepcion	32	29	18	8		
Ydem de Sn Antonio Balero	49	35	36	29		
Totales del Presente Año	438	388	392	291	4	7
Totales del Año anterior	435	385	390	287	4	7
Aumento	3	3	2	4		
Resumen General de Españoles	145	125	246	224		
Ydem de Indios	183	148	26	25		
Ydem de Mestizos	35	25	26	7		
Ydem de color quebrado	75	90	94	35		
Ydem de Esclabos					4	7
Totales	438	388	392	291	4	7
Resumen General de Eclesiasticos Seculares	2					
Ydem de Regulares	6					
Ydem de Casados	330	330				
Ydem de Viudos	38	58				
Ydem de Solteros	62					
Totales	438	388	392	291	4	7

Real Presidio de Sn Antonio de Bexar y Diziembre 31 de 1783.

Manuel delgado   Jose Ignasio de la pena

Nota.

Que para la Formacion de el Estado que Manifiesta el Numero

This census reports the Jurisdiction of Bexar in the Province of Texas, dated at the Royal Presidio December 31, 1783. It shows a population of 1,509 plus 11 slaves—an increase of 3 men, 3 women, 2 boys, 4 girls during the year. Spaniards numbered 740, Indians 382, mestizos 93, and 294 were of "broken color." There were 2 parish priests, 6 friars, 330 married couples, 58 widows, and 62 bachelors. All of which is certified by "Manuel delgado" and "Jose Ignasio de la pena," whose rubrics are bolder than their penmanship.

CHAPTER 4

THE TIRED AND THE INTREPID

Miguel Hidalgo y Costilla

For fifty years after 1776 everything conspired against Spain. British colonies set a bad example when they revolted; the French revolution challenged the ancient Spanish concept of government; Napoleon's invasion of Spain in 1808 brought a six-year civil war and the "corruption of liberalism." In the New World revolutions, filibusters, pirates, and *Americanos* harassed Spain when she was too feeble to deal with them. She plummeted to a third-rate power in half a century.

Texas, northeastern edge of her colonial empire, was vulnerable. While Louisiana was Spanish (1762–1800), even while it was French (1800–1803), border tension eased. But after 1803 when brash, pushing United States bought it—and claimed Texas went with it, too—the border bred constant trouble.

First came enigmatic Philip Nolan. For ten years before the Spaniards stopped him in 1801 he explored Texas, caught horses, traded, and lived with Indians and lounged around San Antonio and Nacogdoches, always protected by a Spanish passport. Suspicion grew, and when he built a stockade near present Waco, Spanish soldiers captured his men, killed Nolan and cut off his ears to send to the governor. Was Nolan plotting to seize Texas, or only trying to make a living as a trader, or was he a secret agent of the United States? Nobody ever knew; but he proved how easily and how far armed men could penetrate into Spanish Texas.

In 1806 United States and Spanish military officials agreed that neither would control the land between the Sabine River and Arroyo Hondo. This Neutral Ground—about forty miles wide—promptly filled up with men who wanted no government and lived by depredation. It was a rendezvous for desperadoes, a recruiting field for filibusters.

Far south of Texas, on September 16, 1810, an idealistic priest and some ambitious young army officers opened the decade-long fight for Mexican independence. Father Miguel Hidalgo, resenting three centuries of Spanish oppression, rallied Indians with a slogan that began by endorsing religion and ended: "Down with bad government! Death to the Spaniards!"

His 80,000 followers terrorized central Mexico, almost took the capital, then broke into guerrilla bands that fought on bravely—or stupidly—for ten years. Father Hidalgo fled toward Texas, and

Peter Ellis Bean kept Nolan's story—and Bean's—alive in his Memoir, *republished many times. He was seventeen when he came to Texas with Nolan. Spaniards kept him prisoner seven years. Released by royalists, he joined Morelos's rebellion as a colonel; fought under Jackson in the Battle of New Orleans; and the next ten years lived briefly in Mexico, Louisiana, Tennessee, Arkansas, and Texas. Thereafter he divided his time between his Mexican wife at Jalapa and his Texas wife at Nacogdoches, where he was Indian agent. He died on his Mexican wife's hacienda in 1846. Neither Texans nor Mexicans held Bean in high regard, but both found him useful on occasion. His principal monument is his own* Memoir. Below: *his home at Nacogdoches.*

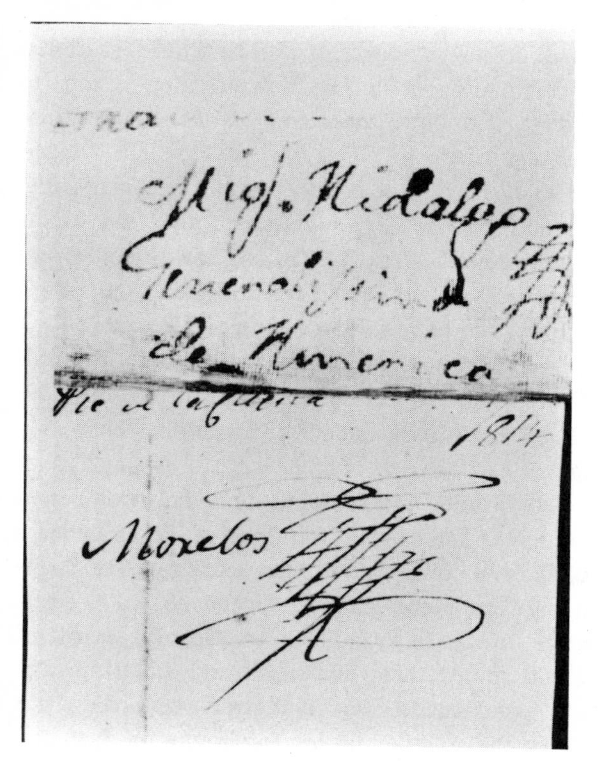

José María Morelos y Pavón led Mexican revolutionists after 1811. This priest declared Mexico independent, drafted a constitution.

Félix María Calleja del Rey, Spanish commander against the rebels, executed Hidalgo in 1811, Morelos in 1815. He was Viceroy 1813–16.

the King's Viceroy continued to rule from Mexico City. In San Antonio a revolutionary seized power in January, 1811, but the Texans who knew and cared little about the Hidalgo movement quickly reinstated the King's officials.

Before Hidalgo's execution (August, 1811) he sent Bernardo Gutierrez de Lara, a blacksmith, through Texas to get aid from the United States. In the Neutral Ground he found fifty men eager to fight anybody. He went on to the United States, gathering moral, financial, and military support.

Death of Morelos.

He found Lieutenant Augustus W. Magee, a West Pointer from Vermont, disgruntled over slow promotion. He commissioned him colonel and himself general, and assembled at Natchitoches a conglomerate army of Americanos, Frenchmen, Mexicans, and Indians.

Gutierrez, a master of florid rhetoric, scattered proclamations calling on downtrodden Texans to aid in their own liberation, while Magee took Nacogdoches in August, 1812. He seized $100,000 worth of goods, traded them across the border for supplies, and issued the first Texas newspaper, *Gaceta de Texas.* Townspeople and turncoat royalists joined his army, and the King's soldiers fell back to San Antonio. The rebels took La Bahía in November, and San Antonio in April. There, April 6, these importers of Liberty declared Texas independent of Spain but "inviolably joined" to Mexico, which was still Spanish!

Magee died at La Bahía, and the incompetent Gutierrez headed this Republic of Texas under a dictatorial constitution. After executing the Spanish governor and sixteen officers the 3,000 liberators broke into factions. A Spanish army of 2,000 routed them in August and killed most of the Americanos; but Gutierrez, who did "not know the number of his forces nor in fact any

GACETA DE TEXAS.

No. 1.] NACOGDOCHES, 25 de MAYO, de 1813.

LA SALUD D. L PUEBLO ES LA SUPREMA LEY.

REFLEXIONES.

Si desde el momento mismo en que empezamos nuestra regeneracion politica hubieramos tratado de establecer de buena fe un sistema, tanto en los asuntos militares como en los que corresponden á la parte civil; si hubieramos sabido aprovechar todos los recursos con que hemos favorecido la justa causa de nuestra libertad é independencia; y en fin, si hubieramos seguido siempre la luz de la recta razon, ya seriamos enteramente

caer baxo barbara dominacion Española. Santa [illegible] Cartagena que disfrutaban ya del mismo bien que Caracas apenas vieron caer otra vez á sus hermanos en la esclavitud, cuando de comun acuerdo marcharon en su [illegible], y sin duda alguna en este mismo momento Venezuela es ya otra vez libre. El Rio de la Plata ofrece el grande espectaculo de una regeneracion feliz y gloriosa. El Perú todo se conmueve, y no tardará en imitar tan bellos y generosos exemplos. La isla de Cuba ancia por el momento de romper los lazos que superficialmente la unen á la España, y tomar parte en la causa comun de la independencia y libertad de la America. Todo esta maduramente convinado: y no la detienen mas que los su-

The Gaceta de Texas, *first Texas newspaper, was written at Nacogdoches but printed in Natchitoches and probably circulated only in the United States.*

part of his business," escaped to plot again. Spain offered a reward for him of 500 pesos dead, 1,000 alive; for other leaders, 250 pesos if brought in by a Protestant, 500 if by a Catholic.

Not one of these liberators was a Texan or concerned about Texas. They were not the stuff of which nations are made. After their foray Spain ordered eviction of all Americanos and Liberals; prohibited trade with Louisiana; and planned once more to colonize Texas with loyal Spaniards. Smuggling continued, the Americanos remained, and no Spaniards came.

In New Orleans, Natchitoches, and Natchez Frenchmen, Americanos, loyal Spaniards and rebel Spaniards—pirates, bandits, merchants, lawyers, land speculators, patriots of all kinds pondered what they might do for Texas and what Texas might do for them. When England and the United States, at war three years, fought their last battle at New Orleans in 1815, the plotters paused long enough to aid the American cause, then resumed their plotting.

Gutiérrez de Lara's seal for Texas is inscribed "Independent Mexico," without mention of Texas.

Safe in the United States, these oddly assorted associates joined with Gulf pirates to "do something about Texas." To help them, Louis Aury, a privateer of many allegiances, declared Galveston a port of the mythical Mexican Republic in 1816, and did good business in goods and Negroes.

In 1817 Jean Laffite supplanted him. A hero of the battle of New Orleans, Laffite since 1810 had been the shiftiest and richest pirate smuggler in the Gulf, with respectable connections in New

Jean Laffite (Lafitte to non-Texans) probably was born in France, but when he was twenty-four he and his brother Pierre were well established in New Orleans as smugglers and privateers, operating throughout the Caribbean. They fought under Jackson in the Battle of New Orleans, then resumed business. Jean established himself on Galveston Island in 1817, raided commerce on the Gulf, and willingly worked for and against the rebels in Mexico, the Spaniards, filibusters, French intruders, and the United States. In 1820 he sailed away—some say to die in Yucatán, some say to reappear under another name as a banker in Kansas City. Pierre was the abler of the Laffite brothers, but Jean was the romantic figure.

Real Orden

Exmo. Sor. = El Rey ha resuelto que á todos los vecinos de la Provincia de la Luisiana q. en virtud de la cesion hecha á la Francia quieran pasar á establecerse en ese Reyno, no se les exijan derechos algunos por los generos efectos y muebles que conduxeren con tal que sean de su uso y no para comerziar, á no justificar haver pagado los derechos y pertenencias antes de la emigracion.

Royal Order of September 24, 1803, opening the door into Texas after the sale of Louisiana to the United States.

Orleans and a resourceful brother, Pierre, to help him. He called his island lair Campeche, organized a government loyal to the "Mexican Republic" with a thousand devoted, villainous subjects, who built forts and warehouses when they were not seizing cargoes in the Gulf to fill them. Laffite lived elegantly in a stranded boat—his *Red House* —enforcing strict discipline but dividing booty fairly, and alternately helping and betraying all comers.

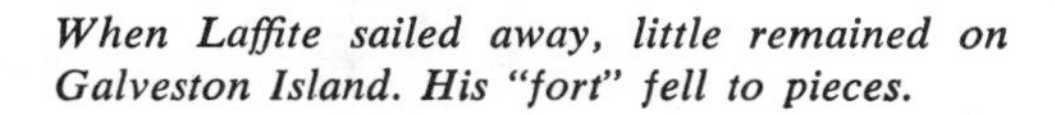

When Laffite sailed away, little remained on Galveston Island. His "fort" fell to pieces.

But the strangest of the visitors to Texas arrived at Galveston early in 1818.

They were members of The Society for the Cultivation of the Vine and Olive who left France after Napoleon fell to become farmers in America. The men had been Napoleon's officers, some were nobles and their wives gentlewomen. They first settled in Alabama on land the United States gave them, but soon moved to a tract in Texas that nobody had said they could have. They brought along plenty of muskets, sabers, and gunpowder but not many implements or seed. Laffite helped them, then alerted the Spanish.

Twenty miles from the mouth of the Trinity the Frenchmen built Champ d'Asile, a fortified pentagon where even the cabins had gun slots. They drilled daily under colonels supervised by two generals, smoked peace pipes with Indians, played parlor games, and swapped war stories. In July, 1818, before planting a vine or a tree, these Frenchmen abandoned their idyllic Texas haven and returned with their women to the United States. Neither Spain nor the Indians nor the United States nor Laffite wanted this oasis of French culture. Governor Martínez's soldiers obliterated Champ d'Asile as De León had La Salle's Fort St. Louis more than a century before. Laffite continued to rule Galveston.

Chasselat Del
Puisse le champ d'Asile cet
anciens cette colonie du Texas fond
puisse la plus héroïque ces résignati
et généreuses de tous les pays et ce
A Paris chez Bulla Rue St. Jacques N° 38. et chez

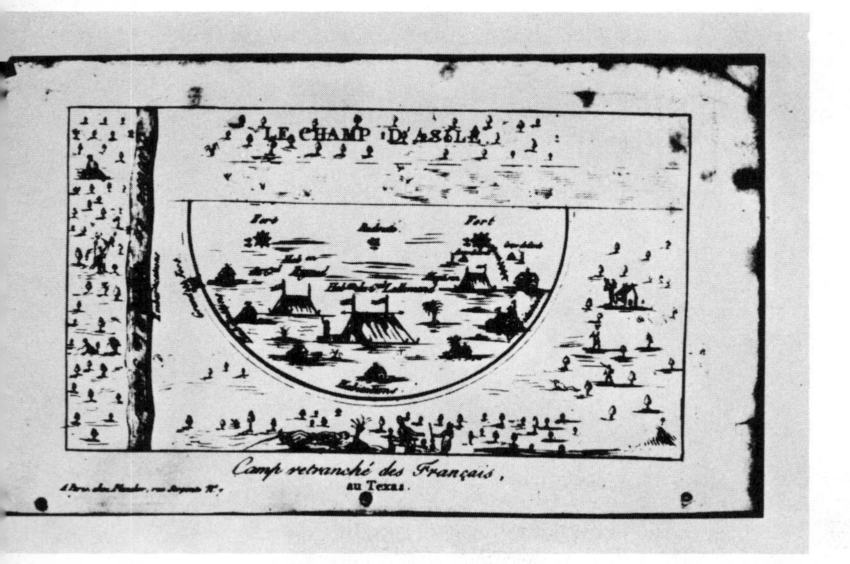

Pomel Sculp.

CHAMP D'ASILE.

-tion d'une origine pure et sans tache, cette retraite dont l'institution le but et le nom rappellent les asiles des héros malheureux, s'accroître et s'embellir par la prospérité et ne plus se recruter par la proscription -as être éprouvée par de nouveaux revers, par de nouvelles tempêtes! tel est le vœu de toutes les âmes nobles -'en doutons pas, sera exaucé. (Extrait du tableau topographique du Texas et du Tombechbe)

-ibraire palais Royal galerie de bois N.os 197 et 198.

Deposé au Bureau des Estampes.

General Long was twenty-six when he marched into Texas, twenty-nine when he died. His wife Jane, a niece of General Wilkinson, remained a Texan until she died in 1880, age eighty-two. She joined him at his "fort" near Galveston in 1820. When he refused to take her on his final (Goliad) expedition, she manned the fort with a small daughter, an infant born after Long's departure, and a Negro nurse. Daily she fired artillery and kept fires going to make Indians and Spaniards believe the place was well garrisoned. Not until June, 1822, when she belatedly learned of her husband's death, did she abandon the place. She became one of Austin's Old Three Hundred, kept hotels at Brazoria and Richmond, and retold the story of the General for sixty years. Old settlers called her "the Mother of Texas."

At Natchez-on-the-Mississippi ambitious, land-hungry, venturesome men were still planning to rid Texas of Spanish oppression and open her rich lands to honest men like themselves. When the United States officially quit claiming Texas to get Florida in 1819, speculators and adventurers assembled in mass meetings and resolved to liberate Texas.

James Long, merchant and self-educated physician, dubbed himself general and led 400 volunteers to Nacogdoches, where in June, 1819, he declared Texas free and himself president. Volunteers were promised 64,000 acres "as soon as the government is settled"; others could buy land as cheap as ten cents an acre. Long published a newspaper in English, *The Texas Republican,* to entice land-hungry Americanos to his hand-made Republic, and deployed his men to forage and evict the Spaniards.

Laffite, delighted that "the spirit of liberty is sprouting," accepted a commission from Long, then betrayed him to the Spaniards. As Governor Martínez's soldiers neared Nacogdoches in September, Long's men fled across the Sabine "as if they were competing for the Stadium Crown," but 44 of them were captured.

Long's fight with the Indians on Galveston Island.

Dear Sir

Monticello May 14. 20

Your favor of the 3d. is recieved and always with welcome. these texts of truth relieve me from the floating falsehoods of the public papers. I confess to you I am not sorry for the non-ratification of the Spanish treaty. our assent to it has proved our desire to be on friendly terms with Spain; their dissent, the imbecility and malignity of their government towards us. [illegible] have placed them in the wrong in the eyes of the world, and that is well. but to us the province of Techas will be the richest state of our union, without any exception. it's Southern part will make more sugar than we can consume and the Red river, on it's North, is the most luxuriant country on earth. Florida, moreover, is our's. every nation in Europe considers it such of right. we need not care for it's occupation in time of peace, and, in war, the first cannon makes it ours without offence to any body. the friendly advisements too of Russia and France, as well as the change of government in Spain, now ensured, require a further and respectful forbearance. while their request will rebut the plea of prescriptive possession, it will give us a right to their approbation when taken in the maturity of circumstances. I really think too that neither the state of our finances, the condition of our country, nor the public opinion urges us to precipitation into war. the treaty has had the valuable effect of strengthening our title to Techas because the cession of the Floridas in exchange for Techas imports an acknolegement of our right to it. this province moreover, the Floridas & possibly Cuba will join us on the acknolegement of their independance, a measure to which their new government will probably accede voluntarily. but why should I be saying all this to you, whose mind all the circumstances of this affair have had possession of for years? I shall rejoice to see you here; and were I to live to see you here finally, it would be a day of Jubilee. but our days are all numbered, & mine are not many. god bless you & preserve you muchos años. Th: Jefferson

Thomas Jefferson had corresponded with Philip Nolan about Spanish Texas and never lost interest in the region. In 1820 he writes President Monroe that "the province of Techas will be the richest state of our union, without any exception."

For more than a year Long shuttled between Louisiana and Galveston, trying to get his republic born. He surrendered the presidency to E. W. Ripley, who never came near Texas, and gave over command of troops to José Trespalacios, who spent his time negotiating instead of fighting. Long built a fort near Galveston, which Laffite had abandoned, and enlisted an army of 52 men. His wife joined him and as Long was moving against La Bahía and San Antonio, their third child was born there.

On October 4, 1821, General Long achieved the only victory of his military career. His 52 men rushed into La Bahía at dawn, firing into the air and yelling like 300 Indians. Everybody fled or took cover. The conquerors waited patiently in the deserted plaza until at last an alcalde ventured warily out. Long grasped him warmly by the hand, assured him all was well, and ordered a salute in his honor. As the cannon fired "one of the gunners fell fainting on the carriage, another had his face burned and . . . a pistol hanging from a third man's belt went off and shot him through the Leg," the startled alcalde reported.

At La Bahía Long learned that Mexico had been independent of Spain for eight months, and that Governor Martínez refused to accept him as a colleague in the cause of liberty. He was imprisoned and six months later was killed by a guard in Mexico City. And thus ends the career of the creator of the second Republic of Texas.

Long's backers and followers, interested in real estate not liberty, prematurely spread the news that Americanos could get free land in Texas. He was the last, and most respectable, of the filibusters. While he was plotting, another Americano was working out the plan that legally and peaceably got Texas land for Americanos.

CHAPTER 5

LAND OF BEGINNING AGAIN

Moses Austin.

Antonio María de Martínez, colonel of His Catholic Majesty's Zamora infantry, had arrived in San Antonio in March, 1817, determined to convert Texas into a strong, prosperous outpost of the empire. A decorated veteran of European wars, a stanch absolutist, he was the last governor Spain ever sent to Texas.

On his way to his new post, he talked Texas with Viceroy Apadoca in Mexico City and with Joaquin de Arredondo, commandant general at Monterrey. The Viceroy, a newcomer himself, thought something could be done for Texas but the hard-bitten General who in his ten years on the frontier had slaughtered Hidalgo's men and quelled more than one rebellion in Texas held out little hope. Texas—its predatory Indians, its handful of lazy colonists, its thieving, undisciplined, unpaid soldiers—Texas was hopeless. Its vastness, its nearness to the United States, made it a magnet for filibusters. If Spanish farmers could be colonized . . . if a Texas port could be opened . . . if the King's treasury were not empty . . . if, in short, the Spanish empire were not an empty shell waiting to be shattered—Arredondo might have been less cynical. Martínez would have to learn, as he had learned, about Texas.

Nothing the new Governor had known in Europe prepared him for what he found in Texas. Conditions appalled him, but his good mind evolved in intervals between filibuster alarms and excursions a solution for every problem. With 2,000 trained soldiers he could build roads and presidios radiating from San Antonio to the coast, to the United States border, into New Mexico, and into north Mexico; he could exterminate hostile Indians, stop smuggling, and make travel safe. If Spaniards would not move to Texas, he would colonize Swiss, Germans, or docile Tlascaltecan Indians. He would make Matagorda a port, to tie Texas economically to the rich center of Mexico. These things and a hundred others he proposed, month after month. None of his plans was approved; money and men never came; no one in authority shared his conviction that Texas was the empire's vital, vulnerable salient.

Then after forty frustrating months he sat listening to an elderly, travel-stained stranger who arrived on a borrowed horse. He unfolded a plan so sensible and workable that the Governor's hopes rose again.

The visitor, vouched for by Baron de Bastrop, said he was Moses Austin, formerly a naturalized subject of His Catholic Majesty who wanted to be a Spaniard again—and bring into Texas 300 Americano families, former Spanish subjects, from the Louisiana territory. They were people of property and would remain permanently to develop the land and fight filibusters, Indians, and all the King's enemies. They would make this Texas wilderness prosperous and safe and it would cost Spain nothing, except vacant land no Mexican would live on.

For Austin this was the last great gamble of a lifetime of speculation on successive frontiers; to Martínez it was a way to make Texas securely Spanish—Arredondo would have to approve it. It was a strange and immediate meeting of minds that took place in the dilapidated governor's palace in grimy San Antonio, two days before Christmas in 1820. However different their backgrounds, Martínez and Austin had things in common; each had been thwarted by uncontrollable circumstances and each refused to accept defeat as long as he could figure out still another plan. For both of them Austin's proposal was an everything-to-gain, nothing-to-lose proposition.

Connecticut-born Austin had pioneered in western Virginia, then for twenty-two years in Missouri. There he had been an important man, the richest in his community—miner, tanner, banker, merchant, importer, and exporter among other things. But the War of 1812 and the Panic of 1819 had broken him and pushed him to this new frontier: "To remain in a Country where I had enjoyed *welth* in a state of *poverty,* I could Not submit to!"

Austin's plight was shared by about half the population of the United States. The panic had wiped out farmers and speculators, closed banks, and ruined business. Before 1820 bankrupt farmers moved farther west to take up government land on a vague promise to pay for it later. But in 1820 Congress ordered cash on the barrelhead—no money, no land. That stopped the normal westward movement; the Land Office sold 5,000,000 acres on credit in 1819; only 750,000 acres for cash in 1821. Spanish Texas was easy to reach, its lands rich. Austin knew that thousands of other men who had to begin again were looking toward Texas; and he calculated that if he could be the man who guided them there—the empresario—he might die solvent, maybe rich.

Martínez approved Austin's proposal, sent it hopefully on to Arredondo, and Austin began a tedious three-month journey home, "undergoing everything but death." He was still en route when his proposal was approved—and when Mexico separated herself from Spain.

Admiral Juan Ruiz de Apodaca, Viceroy, 1816–21, suppressed republican rebellions but was powerless against Iturbide's plan.

The Spanish world had been falling apart since 1808 when Napoleon enthroned his brother in Madrid. From 1810 to 1820 revolutions shook Mexico. The rebels never triumphed but were never crushed, and the Spanish Viceroy kept control of the capital.

But in 1820 incredible things occurred. In Spain an army forced the King to put into effect a liberal constitution that destroyed the ancient privileges of crown, nobles, army and church officers, and great landholders; it democratized the empire and made colonials full Spanish citizens.

In Mexico the privileged classes promptly demanded independence and made common cause with die-hard liberals who had been fighting ten years to make all men equal. This unnatural alliance—reactionaries trying to preserve their privileges and liberals sworn to destroy them—lasted just long enough to free Mexico from Spain. On February 24, 1821, at Iguala, Colonel Augustín de Iturbide of the royal army joined the rebels under Vicente Guerrero in declaring Mexico independent, and the last Spanish viceroy had to agree. Spain lost not only the land Austin sought but all Texas along with Mexico. The colonial

Here in December, 1820, Moses Austin proposed to Governor Martínez the colonization of Americanos in Texas. The palace bore the arms of the Spanish Hapsburgs and the date 1749. For more than half a century the Spanish king's representative had had his official headquarters here.

Kitchen of Governor's Palace, San Antonio.

The Governor's courtyard, considerably improved since Austin's day, is a fine example of Spanish-American domestic architecture.

Agustín de Iturbide, native Mexican, fought independence until 1820, then united discordant factions to achieve it. He was Emperor Agustín I, 1821–23; executed 1824.

Iturbide was of good but not noble family. As emperor he ennobled his kin and devised a royal coat of arms.

Kingdom of New Spain was now the sovereign Mexican nation. While its discordant leaders jockeyed for position, Moses Austin reached home and on June 10, 1821, died.

The land had changed masters. The Empresario was dead. Martínez and Arredondo were out. The story might have ended here, and Texas might today have been little different from the Mexican states south of the Rio Grande.

Juan O'Donojú, last Viceroy, arrived to find Mexico independent. He joined the provisional government.

Exmo. S. TEN. GRAL. D. JUAN O-DONOJÚ
Ultimo Virrey de Nueva España: prestó el Juramento en
en 3. de Agosto de 1821. firmó los tratados de Cordova en 24.

But Moses Austin had a son. This son, Stephen F. Austin, crossed the invisible line between the United States and Texas on July 16, 1821. He was twenty-seven, a bit soft from office work in New Orleans, still dubious of the Texas scheme but duty bound to carry it on, having inherited it —and little else—from his father.

Along the blazed trail called Camino Real he appraised the unbelievably rich and varied virgin land awaiting an awakening touch. The bright redlands of the east, thick with semi-tropical vegetation and taller pines than he had ever seen; rich black soil of central Texas, ideal for cotton and corn; sandy brush country farther west, good for cattle; well-placed creeks and rivers—surely here was a world in itself that could sustain millions of people. But the people had not come. A few squatters lived near Nacogdoches, but until he reached San Antonio he saw no habitations, nowhere a cultivated field or a tended herd; only wild horses, cattle, game, and fowl under the summer sun.

For him this journey was the end of everything he had planned for himself. For almost a year he had been fitting himself to practice law in New Orleans. Two years before he had been a federal judge in Arkansas, planning to settle down as a planter, merchant, and officeholder—he narrowly missed election as territorial delegate to Congress. But these had been makeshift, depression-born objectives, not what he had trained himself for since childhood.

During the years of his father's affluence he had grown up in Spanish-French-American Missouri and been schooled in Connecticut and Kentucky. His versatile father had trained him as an apprentice, then partner, in the myriad Austin enterprises. Stephen was adjutant of his militia company and a member of the Missouri legislature five years.

At twenty-five he thought he was established as a man of business and public affairs; he expected to live out his life in Missouri looking after the family properties and doing his duty as a United States citizen. Then the evil days came. The Austin empire collapsed, and Stephen was on his own.

Now in the summer of 1821 he was on foreign soil, renouncing his citizenship, reluctantly beginning a career for which the very vicissitudes of his life had prepared him. But on the way to San Antonio he thought not of these things but of this marvelous, free land and the thousands of Americanos hungering for it.

He conferred with Governor Martínez, proved his heirship, and planned his colony. He explored the land and read the inquiries that swamped him. Then he saw his father had been right. Texas was the Promised Land. Stephen Austin believed he could settle 1,500 families there as easily as 300. Missouri was "all alive and nothing spoken of but the province of Texas"; his mother believed that "one third of the popolation will move [there] in the cours of another year." New Orleans reported "hundreds on the way and thousands ready to go."

The great news of free land in Texas—really free—was sweeping through the United States as fast as letters, newspapers, and word of mouth could carry it. Everybody who had to move or wanted to move was talking Texas. Men called it Texas Fever.

Austin's colony was along the broad valleys of the Brazos and the Colorado and included the rich land between them. It was the richest region of Texas, and had never been inhabited. To it swarmed immigrants before Austin was ready to receive them—before even the new rulers of Mexico recognized his right to give them land.

Austin's colony was a subdivision of the State of Coahuila y Texas in the Mexican Republic, but Austin performed functions normally done by federal or state officials. His crude, official seal was lettered "Government of Texas." **Right,** *Austin is being summoned to the field against Indians. Deaf Smith, famous scout, is with him.*

OF
AUSTIN

Official seals used in Texas after 1824. Left, *Paymaster's seal used during the years 1824–25.* Below, *Seal of the Supreme Government of the Free State of Coahuila y Texas, which was created in 1824 and functioned, under difficulties, until Santa Anna dissolved it in 1835.* Bottom, *Judicial seal of the District of Austin, of which San Felipe was capital. Note variations of the eagle-cactus-serpent design.*

Félix Fernández, early revolutionist who never surrendered, changed his name to Guadalupe Victoria in fealty to the Virgin of Guadalupe and in confidence of victory. First president of the Republic, he managed to stay in office four years. In the symbolic design, right, *names of states are written on cactus petals, and the cap of Liberty hopefully floats above the eagle. Essential features of the Plan of Iguala by which Iturbide and Vicente Guerrero made Mexico independent, and the first printing of the Federal Constitution of 1824, are shown below.*

Confident that he could get prompt approval in Mexico City, Austin hurried to the capital. He arrived in April, 1822, to find "the whole people and Country still Agitated in the revolutionary Convulsions—public Opinion Vacillating . . . Party spirit raging . . . the recently established Government almost sinking." Nobody had much time for the slender young real-estate agent from Texas.

He waited and learned Spanish while the provisional government gave way to a congress, while Generalísimo Iturbide got himself crowned Emperor Agustín I (and last), and while "a General Santana," as Austin understood the name, toppled the Emperor from his shaky, homemade throne to make Mexico a republic. To each short-lived administration Austin presented his case; more than once he got what he asked, but the next group voided it.

A year of patient persistence finally got him what he had expected to obtain in two weeks, authority to settle Americanos in Texas. It gave him more: an understanding of the realities of Mexican politics and personal acquaintance with men who would determine Texas' future. He came back with an understanding of the psychology of the new masters of Mexico as well as of their language.

Guadalupe Victoria, first president of Mexico, 1824–28.

Extracto del Plan

1º La Religion C.A.R. si...

2º La absoluta Independ.a

3º Gobierno monarquico, ...
analoga al Paiz

4º Fernando 7º y en su cas...
nante seran los Emp...
narca ya hecho, y pre...
ambicion

5º Habrá una Junta inter...
efectivo este Plan

6º Esta se nombrará gube...
Vocales ya propuesto...

7º Governará en virtud de...
Rey, é interin este ...
y hasta entonces se...
ordenes

8º Si Fernando no resolvi...
Regencia mandará...
se resuelva la terc...

9º Será sostenido este Gobi...
tido

10 Las Cortes resolveran si se há de continuar esta Junta, ó

CONSTITUCION

FEDERAL

DE LOS ESTADOS UNIDOS

MEXICANOS.

Sancionada por el Congreso General Constituyente, el 4. de Octubre de

1824.

Imprenta del Supremo Gobierno de los Estados unidos mexicanos, en Palacio.

In Texas during Austin's eighteen-month absence immigrants continued to arrive but many stopped off in Arkansas and Louisiana to await developments. Makeshift arrangements for settling them and keeping order, fear that Mexico would never give them land, caused many to return to the States. Those who remained had a hard time. Drought, Indian raids, only deer and horse meat to eat, no bread, no vegetables—these were bad enough; but there was always the fear that Mexico would evict them. Somehow about two hundred families stuck it out until Austin returned in August, 1823, with good news.

Party dress of Mrs. Elizabeth Seward, an Austin colonist, shows that all was not buckskin and homespun in early Texas. Dress is green lutestring plaid silk in Godey's style.

"Texas" had been an indefinite term since Spanish days and it continued so under Mexico. In the region between the Nueces (modern Corpus Christi) and the Sabine (Louisiana boundary) colonists from the United States settled after 1821. This map shows the principal colonial tracts and the location of modern towns. Omitted are grants in which few or no settlements were made. The valleys of the Colorado and Brazos rivers received most of the early colonists who sought rich bottom land. Austin's pre-eminence as a colonizer is indicated by the large areas granted to him.

Married men could have 4,600 acres. Austin's only charge was twelve-and-a-half cents an acre for surveying, recording, and issuing title, which many objected to paying. The colonist selected his land, Austin's surveyor mapped it, then Austin and the land commissioner signed the deed. Austin had to certify that each man had become a Mexican citizen and was a Catholic, and was of good character. He gave deeds to 272 families by September, 1824.

For five years Austin was the supreme executive, judicial, legislative, and military authority, without salary or expense account. Only he could give land to foreigners; his house in San Felipe, not the Governor's palace in San Antonio, was the center of this bustling new Texas.

Twenty-four other men got empresario contracts and Austin got four more. The map of Texas was covered with names of men who agreed to settle a hundred or more families. An optimist would have expected Texas to be thickly populated within a decade, but only Austin and Green DeWitt, whose grant was around Gonzales, had much success.

Empresario Austin and his land commissioner, Baron de Bastrop, issue land deeds at San Felipe de Austin to assorted settlers in Texas.

Texas and Coahuila formed a single state in the Mexican Republic. In the twelve-man legislature Texas had one, then two, and finally three representatives. A Mexican *jefe político* (deputy governor) lived at San Antonio, but local government in the colonies was in the hands of Americanos. Each community elected its *ayuntamiento* (council), headed by an alcalde and staffed by officers whose titles few could pronounce. These new Mexican citizens knew little about what went on elsewhere in their adopted country. They were busy clearing their land, tending their crops, and inviting kinsmen in the States to share the wonders of Texas. Communication southward was slow and uncertain and the colonists were content to attend to their own affairs. And for a few years statesmen in Mexico City heard and cared little about the people who were taming their northeastern frontier.

At Peach Point, near the home of his sister, Mrs. Bryan, Austin built this farm home.

Austin spent most of his time in his log house at San Felipe de Austin, colony capital.

Well used by Austin's colonists.

THE TEXAS GAZETTE.

PRINTED AND PUBLISHED WEEKLY, BY GODWIN BROWN COTTEN, AT SIX DOLLARS, PER ANNUM, IN ADVANCE.

VOL. 1. AUSTIN, TEXAS, FRIDAY, SEPT. 25, 1829. NO. 1.

PROSPECTUS.

THE benefit which a community derives from periodical publications, are too well known to require us to enumerate them.

The Gazette will be dedicated to political and miscellaneous intelligence.—It will chronicle events as they transpire within our own country, or may come to us from foreign parts.

This Republic, just rising into importance, is now assuming a proud stand among the nations of the world, and basing her institutions on the immutable principles of CIVIL LIBERTY, will guarantee to its citizens the enjoyment of their political rights.

This paper will be the advocate of the National and State constitutions; and of harmony and union. No communications or paragraphs containing personalities of any description whatever, will ever be admitted into its columns, neither will they be open to the virulent or abusive effusions of party spirit. The Editor will spare no pains to procure translations of the laws passed by the Legislature, and such other acts of the Government as may be important, and he flatters himself that the public will derive much valuable information on these subjects, which the want of a press has heretofore rendered it difficult to procure.

A few years ago, and this colony was almost unknown to civilized man, but the indefatigable exertions of Colonel S. F. Austin has brought about this desirable end. And indeed, through his fostering it is now rapidly rising to importance. And we will from time to time, communicate such information as will be useful to emigrants and promote the prosperity of the country.

The Editor has undertaken a difficult task—The uncertainty of receiving regular intelligence by mail he will endeavor to overcome, by a correspondence with New-Orleans.

The Spaniard has invaded our country, but in numbers so insignificant that if the people are true to themselves,he will not be able to advance ten leagues into the interior. It will be the duty of the Editor to keep you well informed of the events of the war.

TERMS.

☞ The price of subscription will be $6 per annum—payable at any time after the first number has been issued in CASH or PRODUCE.—Advertisements of not more than ten lines will be published for $1 for the first, and fifty cents for each subsequent insertion.

MILITIA LAW.

Passed 23d June, 1828.

The Governor of the State of Coahuila and Texas to all its Inhabitants—Know Ye, that the Congress of said state have decreed as follows:—

No. 58.—The Constitutional Congress of the free, independent and sovereign state of Coahuila and Texas have enacted the following

REGULATIONS,

FOR THE NATIONAL MILITIA OF THE STATE.

CHAPTER I.

ARTICLE 1.—It being the duty of every citizen of the state to defend his country when called on to do so, the National Militia shall be comprised of every citizen, from the age of eighteen to fifty years.

ART. 2.—The Militia shall be subject to the orders of the Governor when employed in the service of the state, and to those of the President of the Republic when called out in the service of the nation.

ART. 3.—It shall be composed of infantry and cavalry.

ART. 4.—The infantry shall be organized in battalions, and the cavalry in squadrons.

ART. 5.—Each battalion of infantry shall consist of from four to eight companies. The force of each company shall be one captain, two lieutenants, two sub-lieutenants, one first sergeant, four second sergeants, ten corporals, two drummers, one fifer and from eighty-three, to one hundred and twenty-five privates.

ART. 6.—The staff of the battalion shall consist of one colonel, one lieutenant colonel, one first adjutant, with the rank of captain and grade of third chief of the battalion, one second adjutant with the rank of sub-lieutenant, one chaplain, one surgeon, one armorer, and one drum major.

ART. 7.—A squadron shall consist of two companies, the force of each one of which, shall be one captain, two lieutenants, two ensigns, one first sergeant, four second sergeants, four first corporals, four second corporals, two buglemen, and from seventy-five to one hundred dragoons.

ART. 8.—The staff of the squadron of cavalry in conformity with the 10th article of the national law, of 29th December last, shall consist of one commandant, one adjutant, with the rank of lieutenant, who shall discharge the duties of first adjutant, and one first sergeant-major, who shall discharge the duties of standard-bearer.

ART. 9.—The force of the militia of the state shall consist of three battalions of infantry, five squadrons of cavalry, and six separate companies of cavalry.

ART. 10.—The corps and companies mentioned in the last article shall be formed in the several departments of the state in the following manner, to wit:—one battalion of infantry, one squadron and one separate company of cavalry in the department of Texas: three squadrons and two separate companies of cavalry in the department of Monclova, and two battalions of infantry and two seperate companies of cavalry in the department of Leona Vicario.

ART. 11.—Of the two battalions of infantry assigned to the department of Leona Vicario, one shall be formed in the city of Leona Vicario and village of Villalongin, and the other in the town of Parras and its jurisdiction—one of the separate companies of cavalry shall be formed in the vally of Capelania and the other in Alamo de Parras.

ART. 12.—The three squadrons and three separate companies of cavalry assigned for the department of Monclova shall be formed as follows; one squadron in the city of Monclova and town of Abasolo: one in San Buenaventura and Nadadores, and the other in Guerrero, and there shall be formed a separate company of cavalry in each of the towns of Santa Rosa, Candela and Cienegas.

ART. 13.—The battalion of infantry, squadron and separate company of cavalry of the department of Texas shall be formed as follows, to wit: the battalion shall be formed in Austin and Nacogdoches, the squadron in Bexar and its jurisdiction, and the separate company in Goliad, (formerly Bahia.—*Note*—By a subsequent arrangement, the battalion of Austin and Nacogdoches have been separated and a battalion formed in each.)

ART. 14—In the department of Texas this force will be augmented as the *Empresarios* introduce settlers under their contracts.

ART. 15.—The respective quotas of the corps and companies which have to be formed out of different municipalities will be designated by the governor, agreeably to their population.

ART. 16.—Should there be an overplus of men subject to militia duty, after forming the corps established by the 9th Art. they shall be also organized.

ART. 17.—Special care shall be taken in organizing the corps and companies mentioned in the 10th to the 15th Articles, so that each shall be completed within its own municipality, when the population will admit of it, so as not to divide a corps between two distinct municipalities.

ART. 18.—The fractions that may remain shall be organised into platoons, and third and half companies in the manner presented in the following articles.

ART. 19.—A fraction composed of from ten to fifteen infantry shall form a platoon to be commanded by one first corporal: from fifteen to twenty-five privates shall form the third of a company and have one sub-lieutenant, one sergeant and two corporals: from twenty-five to forty shall form the half of a company and have one first lieutenant, one sub-lieutenant, one first sergeant, one second sergeant, five corporals and one drummer: from forty to eighty shall compose the two thirds of a company and one sub-lieutenant, one second sergeant and one corporal shall be added: and when the number of privates exceed eighty, a full company shall be formed with the officers so prescribed in the 5th Article.

ART. 20.—The fractions of cavalry not exceeding twenty men, shall be commanded by one sergeant and one corporal: from twenty to thirty shall form the third of a company with one ensign, one first sergeant and two second corporals: forty privates shall form the half of a company, and one lieutenant, one second sergeant, one first corporal and one bugleman shall be added; over seventy privates shall form a full company, with the same officers as prescribed by Article 7.

ART. 21.—The fractions of companies, whether infantry or cavalry, can be annexed to the respective corps and separate companies, as the population of the municipality or circumstances may require.

CHAPTER II.

OF THE DUTIES OF THE MILITIA.

ART. 22.—It is the duty of the militia to sustain the independence of the nation, and the federal constitution; to guard and escort prisoners and the public money of the nation, where there are no permanent or active troops, agreeably to the 4th article of the national militia law.

ART. 23.—Whenever the militia are employed for the purposes designated in the foregoing article, or in any other manner, in the service of the nation, they shall be subject to the orders of the President of the Republic, and will receive the compensation corresponding to their class and arms, agreeably to the provisions of the 33d and 35th Articles of the national law.

ART. 24.—Whenever the government calls for a part, or all of the militia to march out of the state, the governor shall notify the legislature, or in its recess, the permanent deputation of the same.

ART. 25.—In the interior service of the state it shall be the duty of the militia—1st. to sustain the constitution of the state, a[illegible] to stand guard at the hall of the legislature while in [illegible]sion; 2d. to furnish patrols, both in the country an[illegible] towns, whenever they are deemed necessary by t[illegible] [illegible]vil authority to preserve the public tranquility, an[illegible] [illegible]nerally to support and defend the civil authority, [illegible] cases whenever called upon to do so; 3d, to pa[illegible] on days of public rejoicings, where there are no troo[illegible] when the civil authority may deem it proper to call them out; 4th, to pursue and apprehend within the limits of their districts, all deserters, vagabonds, thieves, or other evil-doers or criminals, when there are no permanent troops to do it, or when such troops cannot furnish the aid required with the necessary promptness; 5th, to guard and escort in the absence of permanent troops, all prisoners, money or property of the state, from one town to the next, where there is militia to take charge of them, and should there not be a sufficiency of militia for the escort, in the town or place where it ought to be furnished, all there shall be employed, and the necessary number shall be completed out of the escort which came on from the last place, to be selected by lot, and these shall be relieved at the first town or place where there is militia to do it. The militia who go out of the limits of their municipality to escort prisoners or funds of the state, shall be compensated agreeably to the service they perform, out of the militia funds, and the sums which is proved by the necessary vouchers, have been spent for these objects, shall be replaced to the militia fund, out of the public treasury.—6th, to defend the settlements of the respective militia districts throughout their whole extent, whether interior or exterior.

ART. 26.—No militiaman shall be prevented from

The Texas Gazette *began publication at San Felipe de Austin in September, 1829. Its columns were filled with official notices.*

Mary Austin Holley was the "first lady ambassador at large" of Texas. Cousin of the Empresario, widow of a famous educator, she published in 1833 her Texas, Observations, Historical, Geographical, and Descriptive, *followed by her* Texas *(1836), which explained the Revolution and stimulated immigration. She and Austin planned to marry and had selected a home site near the present capital, named in his honor years later.*

TEXAS.

kitchen; the rest are used for bed-rooms, sitting-rooms, &c. indiscriminately. The living cannot but be excellent in a country, which is furnished with such a profusion of the good things of life as Texas. Vegetables of every descriptions, wild fowl, and other game, beef, pork, venison, fowls, butter, eggs, milk, &c., with tea, coffee, and all the like comforts commonly found upon the tables in our country. Unfortunately, cooks do not grow upon trees. The epicure, therefore, who brings with him his morbid appetites, must also bring his cook. But he who can relish the most wholesome viands, dressed in the plain manner of the country, will never find opportunity to complain of the quality or quantity of fare which is to be found upon a Texas table.

The ordinary dress of the inhabitants is fully equal, if not superior, to that of the back-woods settlers of the Western United States. A stranger would be astonished to see, in this infant settlement, a taste and luxury displayed by females in the article of dress, which would compare with that of the old settlements of our country. Dry good stores, well supplied, are to be found in all the towns of much size, and there is, hence, no difficulty to the opulent farmer or mechanic—and opulence is an unfailing consequence of industry here—to supply themselves with the very best articles of clothing. Indeed, no new country in America presents a population more tasteful and genteel in dress than Texas; and one would sup-

From Mary Austin Holley's TEXAS.

Immigration increased the miserable 3,000 Texans in 1820 to 10,000 by 1830, and 20,000 more came during the next five years. And the newcomers were transforming the region psychologically as well as physically. No longer a sterile land of defeat and frustration, Texas was evolving into a bustling, forward-looking province, more like a frontier community of the United States than any in Mexico.

All sorts and conditions of men, from everywhere and for every reason, found their way into Mexican Texas. Singly or in companies, by land and by sea, with or without permission, they sought free land. Some were veterans of other frontiers who loved the adventure of taming new country; most were farmers wiped out in the panic who had to begin again somewhere; a few were professional men who had personal reasons for wanting a new field of action. From all parts of the Union they came to Texas, most of them from the South but many from New York, Pennsylvania, New England, and the Midwest. And there were a few Europeans—French, German, Scandinavian, English, Irish, Polish—to whom Texas had a romantic or practical appeal.

Austin set a high standard: "No frontiersman who has no other occupation than that of a hunter will be received. No drunkard, nor gambler, nor profane idler, nor any man against whom there is even probable grounds of suspicion that he is a bad man." Undesirables were publicly whipped and "exiled" to the United States, their property confiscated.

Other empresarios were more lenient, and doubtless many lawbreakers fled to Texas to escape punishment and remain wicked. "G. T. T." (Gone to Texas) was the standard explanation of the whereabouts of a man who was in trouble. Some fugitives became prominent citizens, a few met Judge Lynch.

Solvent, large-scale planters, such as Jared Groce, came too. Groce, who had operated vast plantations in the Old South, received ten sections of Texas land "on account of the property he has brought with him." He moved in a caravan of fifty covered wagons, his herds of cattle, sheep, horses, and hogs tended by his 100 slaves, from Alabama to the Brazos Valley in 1822. His plantations were fabulous in early Texas. Squads of armed slaves hunted deer and game for his table; he had a resident physician; and visitors slept in guest-houses near his big house at Bernardo.

Jared E. Groce arrived in 1821 from Alabama with 100 slaves to establish great plantations and in 1828 the first cotton gin.

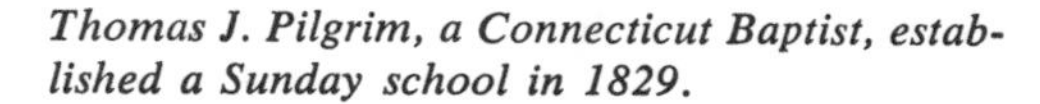

Thomas J. Pilgrim, a Connecticut Baptist, established a Sunday school in 1829.

Most of the newcomers were content with log cabins near a stream and a wearisome diet of dried beef sopped in honey, until they could make a few crops and do better. Little towns sprang up at crossroads and along the rivers, not much to look at but containing surprising amenities. They almost all could boast such niceties as a barbershop, a billiard parlor, and a race track in addition to the inevitable general store and saloons which Texans called groceries. Some towns had a physician or two and several lawyers, who never quite mastered the Code of Mexico but knew how to examine land titles, draw contracts, and sue.

Travelers found the Texans hospitable and generally honest. "I went all through the country, unarmed and unharmed," wrote one. Another said, "Even men who have been expatriated for fear of justice" do not shield criminals; and "money would be as safe without lock and key as in our own country." Stores were seldom locked, homes never.

Thomas J. Pilgrim, an itinerant teacher who knew more Texans than most colonists, admitted "there were some rude and illiterate people among them . . . some were vicious and depraved, but what there was of evil you saw on the surface, for there was no effort at concealment."

For nearly ten years—until 1830—the individualistic, resourceful colonists were content in their new homes. Life was better for them than it had been in the States. They paid no taxes, suffered no foreclosures, and the unstable Mexican government was more remote from them than kinfolk across the Sabine.

CHAPTER 6

CROSS GRAIN

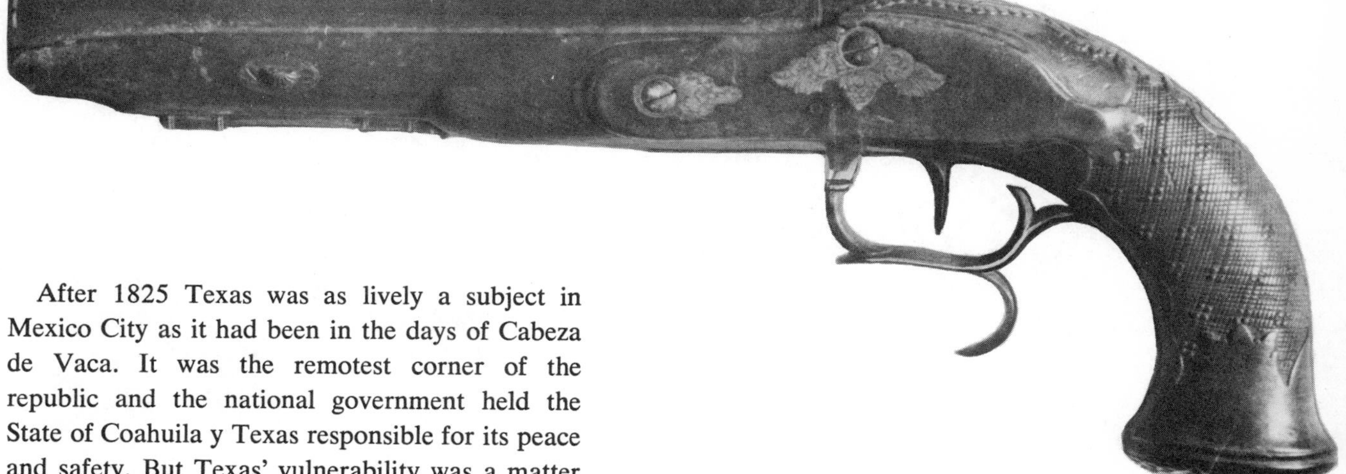

After 1825 Texas was as lively a subject in Mexico City as it had been in the days of Cabeza de Vaca. It was the remotest corner of the republic and the national government held the State of Coahuila y Texas responsible for its peace and safety. But Texas' vulnerability was a matter of national concern—the United States bordered it on two sides. By taking lands that once were Spanish, the Colossus of the North had reached the edge of Texas. Now Texas was filling up with pushing Americanos.

In 1825 the United States proposed that Mexico sell Texas to her. In 1826 came the Fredonian Rebellion at Nacogdoches, near the international line. Mexican statesmen couldn't know that less than sixty men were involved and they had been promptly evicted by bona-fide settlers, leaving behind only a bedraggled red-and-white banner. They did know that the rebellion was headed by the brother of a Texas empresario, that he declared Texas independent, and promised to divide the land with the Cherokees. And they knew the rebels came from the United States, and fled back there—maybe to plot again.

There was not much reassurance in the thinking of the Yankee secretary of state that since Americanos in Texas hold to *"our* principles of law, liberty, and religion" other collisions "may be anticipated with confidence," by way of asking Mexico again to transfer Texas to the United States. The purchase offer was renewed in 1829. In truth, articulate Americans still believed that the Louisiana Purchase included Texas, although the claim was officially abandoned in 1819; and many statesmen, eager to assist Manifest Destiny, coveted the honor of adding Texas to the national domain.

Old Stone Fort at Nacogdoches, officially la Casa Piedra, *built by Gil Ybarbo in 1779, sheltered Nolan's men, Gutierrez and Magee, Long's Texas Republic, the Fredonians, and a court of the Republic of Texas. It now stands on the Stephen F. Austin College campus.*

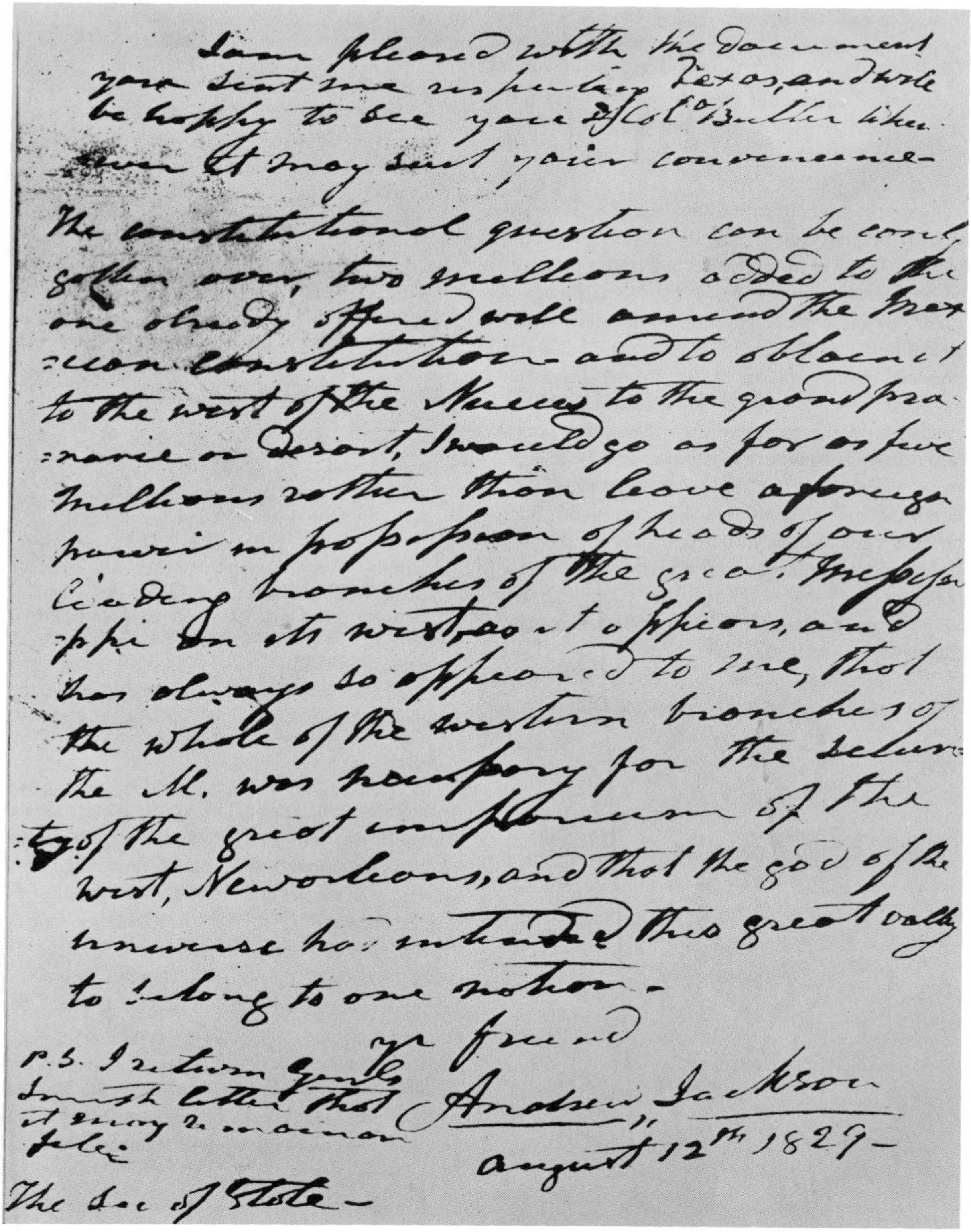

I am pleased with the document you sent me respecting Texas, and will be happy to see you & Col^o Butler whenever it may suit your convenience-

The constitutional question can be easily gotten over, two millions added to the one already offered will amend the Mexican constitution - and to obtain it to the west of the Nueces to the grand prarie or desert, I would go as far as five millions rather than leave a foreign power in possession of heads of our leading branches of the great Mississippi on its west, as it appears, and has always so appeared to me, that the whole of the western branches of the M. was necessary for the security of the great emporium of the west, Neworleans, and that the god of the universe had intended this great valley to belong to one nation-

yr friend

Andrew Jackson

august 12th 1829-

P.S. I return Genl Smith letter that it may be on your file

The Sec of State-

Andrew Jackson was not so coy about Texas in 1829 as he was later.

Mexico had no intention of giving up Texas. Perhaps she should never have "invited" Americanos into the province; certainly she should have Mexicanized them after they came. Whatever her past sins of omission, the time had come for Mexico to integrate Texas into the nation—or let it drift or be plucked away.

First the actual conditions in Texas were studied on the ground and the border patrolled. In 1828 General Manuel Mier y Terán, ostensibly on a scientific exploration, wrote from Nacogdoches: "Texas could throw the whole nation into revolution. . . . The colonists murmur against the political disorganization of the frontier, and the Mexicans complain of the superiority and better education of the colonists. . . . The whole population here is a mixture of strange and incoherent parts without parallel in our federation . . . honorable and dishonorable alike travel with their political constitutions in their pockets, demanding the privileges, authority and officers which such a constitution guarantees." Terán estimated ten Americanos for every Mexican and "the incoming stream of settlers is unceasing."

General Manuel de Mier y Terán, who wrote to Austin, "The affairs of Texas are understood by none but you and me," died in 1832, as tension mounted.

The time for action had come and, with Terán's report before it, the Mexican Congress on April 6, 1830, enacted a law to Mexicanize Texas before it was too late. Americanos already in Texas could remain, but no more could enter. Mexican families and ex-convicts would be planted among the Americanos at public expense. Customs officers would be sent to collect taxes the colonists had never been asked to pay. Additional garrisons of trained soldiers would enforce the new order. Half a million pesos—more than Mexico had spent on Texas in the ten years of colonization—was appropriated to carry the Law of April 6 into effect. Texas belonged to Mexico and at that moment Mexican lawmakers were determined to keep it.

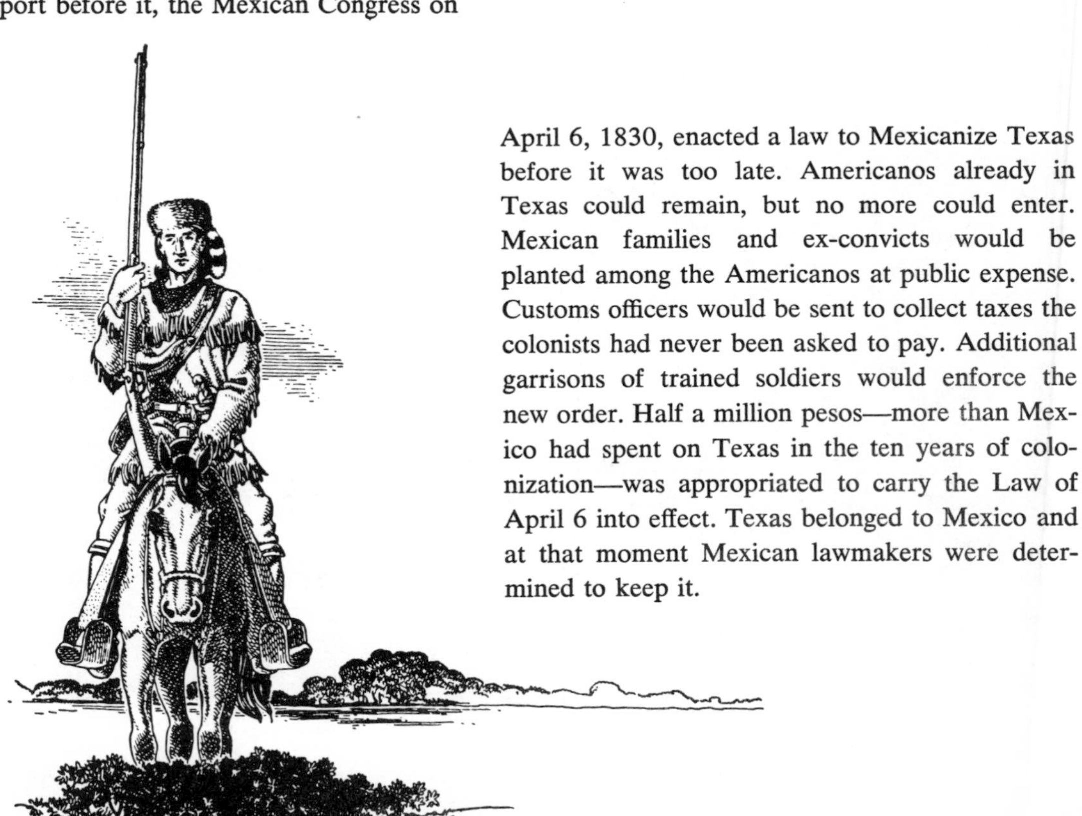

George Fisher was a Texan from 1829 until 1850. First a hated custom officer, then empresario, militia officer, city official, and Masonic leader, he was born in Europe and died in California.

Anastacio de Bustamante, physician and soldier, had fought on both sides in the Mexican Revolution and had been military commandant of the Texas region. As President he signed the Law of April 6, 1830. Texans disapproved of him.

But Mexico could not focus long on Texas. Political instability, which began with independence, increased. Politics was more a matter of *plans, pronunciamentos, cuartelazos* (barracks revolts), and conspiracy than of platforms and ballots. President Victoria, who sent Terán to inspect Texas, left office in 1829—the only early president to surmount revolts till the end of his term. The army pushed aside the man elected to succeed him in favor of Vicente Guerrero. After eight troubled months Vice President Bustamante ousted—and executed—him. Bustamante, who knew the frontier and Texas firsthand, signed the Law of April 6 but was too busy thwarting plots against him to concentrate on far-off Texas during the two years he managed to remain in the Presidency. Texas was never his major problem.

The Law of April 6 seemed just and reasonable to the men who wrote it, but to the Texans it was as a breach of contract. They reacted, as Americanos always do, by grumbling, arguing, and assembling to draft petitions. The mutual oblivion of the Texans and the Mexican government quickly gave way to mutual distrust.

Mexican garrisons encircled the settlements and customs officers began for the first time collecting import taxes, as provided by the Law of April 6. To Anahuac came Colonel John Davis Bradburn, a Kentucky adventurer in Mexican service, a tactless, irascible man whom even Austin pronounced incompetent "and half crazy part of the time." He dissolved an *ayuntamiento,* stopped the issuance of land titles, declared martial law, and jailed a few Texans, among other things.

Armed colonists rushed to Anahuac and on June 13, 1832, while awaiting a cannon to use against Bradburn, signed the Turtle Bayou Resolutions. They declared their "deepest interest and solicitude" for the success of the current Mexican revolution and pledged their "lives and fortunes to . . . the distinguished leader [Santa Anna] . . . so gallantly fighting in defense of civil liberty." These Texans knew nothing about Santa Anna or his principles; they only knew he was trying to oust Bustamante—Bustamante who signed the Law of April 6 and sent Bradburn to harass them. If Santa Anna won, these resolutions would prove Texas' devotion to him; if Bustamante won, no mention more need be made of them.

Colonel Piedras hurried from Nacogdoches to Anahuac and terminated the trouble by letting the Texans out of jail, shipping Bradburn and his soldiers back to Mexico, and telling the Texans to go home. After some bloodletting along the Brazos, all the Mexican garrisons marched out of Texas. By the end of summer in 1832 not a soldier remained to watch the Americanos.

The news from Texas alarmed both the beleaguered government and the rebel Santa Anna. The president could spare none of his dwindling army, but Santanista Colonel Mexia hurried up from Matamoros with 400 soldiers to discipline the Texans. He found no rebellion. The Texans who had sent the garrisons packing swore they were only opposing the tyrant Bustamante. They were all good Santanistas, like Mexia. They gave him a "large, cheerful, and convivial" banquet, showed him the Turtle Bayou Resolutions, and in a week he was back at work below the Rio Grande, convinced that the Texans were loyal to Mexico—and to Santa Anna.

But the Law of April 6 was still law, and the Texans wanted it repealed. As they would have done in the United States, they met in convention to petition the government. Fifty-six elected delegates—no native Mexican, no San Antonian among them—met at San Felipe October 1, 1832, and respectfully asked repeal of the Law of April 6 and statehood for Texas. They asked other things, too—tax exemption, free immigration, use of English in public business, public schools—but repeal and statehood were indispensables.

While Texans were spelling out what they wanted—and learning that unauthorized conventions were illegal in Mexico—their great and good friend Santa Anna was getting himself elected president without difficulty. He had made and unmade governments for ten years; it was now time for him to rule the country personally. April 1, 1833, was inauguration day.

That day a stranger of heroic mold sat with 54 Texans in San Felipe. He was Sam Houston, former militia general, late governor of Tennessee, lately resident in the Cherokee Nation. He represented Nacogdoches in this second Texas Convention, and he seemed to know better than the colonists what they should do. The petitions of last year were readopted without argument and, at Houston's insistence, a constitution was written for a Mexican State of Texas. Austin was sent, at his own expense, to get Santa Anna's approval.

Austin arrived in Mexico in July to find Santa Anna on leave to quell rebellion and Acting President Farías unwilling to act on Texas petitions. After waiting three months Austin, his nerves brittle and "so weary that life is hardly worth having," told Farías that Texans would organize their state, with or without permission. Farías lectured Austin on his manners and showed him the door. Austin wrote men in San Antonio urging them to set up the new state. Soon Austin and Farías were friends again and Santa Anna returned to his office long enough to agree to nearly all the Texans asked, except statehood.

Austin started home December 10, happy that he had removed the major causes of unrest in Texas. He went by Saltillo to pay his respects to the new *comandante general* and brief him on Texas affairs. But that letter he had sent to San Antonio in "irritation and impatience" had gone through channels to the President's office where it was pronounced near-treason and a warrant issued for Austin's arrest.

The General at Saltillo received Austin politely on January 3, 1834, then arrested him and sent him back to Mexico City under guard.

S.A.S. ANTONIO LOPEZ DE SANTA-ANNA

General Martín Perfecto de Cos was sent to Texas by Santa Anna in 1835 to quell the rebellion. He was evicted from Bexar in 1835, returned in 1836, was captured at San Jacinto, but lived to fight Texans again in 1846–47. Santa Anna was his brother-in-law. Below, *Cos's house at San Antonio.*

While Austin languished nearly two years, Santa Anna transformed the Mexican federation into a centralized dictatorship with states, municipalities, everything, controlled by El Presidente. Austin commented that in Mexico politics resembled "its geological features—all is volcanic," and prediction was like saying "when Vesuvius will or will not explode." Opposition to the new regime was widespread but Santa Anna quickly suppressed it. In the north he crushed the rebels in Zacatecas and plundered their state capital; then sent his brother-in-law, General Martin Perfecto de Cos to Saltillo to arrest the governor of Coahuila y Texas and disperse the legislature.

That done, Cos moved his army to San Antonio, the better to watch the Texans. They had not yet defied El Presidente, but they were resisting customs collectors and showing disrespect to the military. Americanos were still flocking there —and no Mexican colonists were arriving.

While the Texans fumed, patient Austin languished in Mexico City.

TO THE GENERAL CONGRESS

OF THE UNITED MEXICAN STATES.

The Ayuntamiento of Austin would respectfully approach the Congress of the nation on the subject of the imprisonment of STEPHEN F. AUSTIN the delegate of Texas, to the National Congress asking for the erection of that province into a separate state of the Republic. The right of approaching the National Congress and asking for a redress of grievances, they have ever been taught to consider as one of the most invaluable guarantees of the Constitution and any invasion of that right should be regarded by all the true friends of freedom, with feelings of just alarm, and as giving cause for just complaint. Was the imprisonment and trial of Stepher

eration, this Ayunta
him and the law.
only on him, it wou
gant indelicacy to
derstood not to be
are correctly inforr
to of Bexar, & beat
that accusation we
have too high an op
ciary, to believe tha
be tortured into a
danger to Colonel A

If any wrong has been committed it has not been by Colonel Austin—If any treason has been intended the whole people of Texas alone are guilty. He represented in his letter their feelings and intentions at the time he was dispatched to Mexico; and if he erred or violated any law, or was wanting in proper respect, or attachment to the government, the people of Texas should alone be the sufferers.—But the people of Texas repel with indignation the charge of treason, and they deny that in either word or deed they ever contemplated any measure unwarranted by what they conceived their Constitutional privileges. They indeed proposed to organize and they have always conceived that they had an undoubted right to do so. But for what would they organize? Not for the purpose of resistance to the government—Not to dismember themselves from the Mexican Republic; for if the question was put to the vote of the people their answer would be unanimous *nollumus mutari.* But that they might present themselves through their representatives in the city of Mexico and add to the Republic a State calculated to be its pride and strength; and inhabited by a people, who, rocked in the cradle of liberty, had been taught from lisping infancy that he who received the protection of a government was bound to aid in sustaining its sovreignty and independence; and that he who meditated differently was a traitor to that country, and would be a villian among his fellow beings. The American character is not correctly understood abroad; they are not of a revolutionary dispositon! No people are more ardently and more affectionately attached to liberty, order, and a faithful observance of law.—No people are more unrelenting and determined in their opposition to usurpation and oppression. Hold out to the people of Texas the Olive branch of peace; convince them that their wants are considered, and their rights protected in the counsels of the Nation, and the voice of complaint will be hushed; and they will rise as one man and swear to rally under no flag save that of the Mexican Nation, to know no government save that of their adopted country.

In conclusion, this Ayuntamiento for itself and the people of this jurisdiction, and speaking the sentiments of the whole united people would respectfully request that Stephen F. Austin be discharged and permitted to return to his constituents. The grant of this request it is not conceived will interfere with the course of justice or be incompatible with the honor and character of the Mexican Nation; but will furnish to the people of Texas renewed evidence that the reign of despotism has ceased, and that all their just and reasonable requests will receive considerate attention from the ruling authorities of the country.—God and liberty.

R. M. WILLIAMSON, Pres't.

W. BARRET TRAVIS, Sec'y.

San Felippe de Austin, 28th, April, 1834.

"The American character is not correctly understood abroad; they are not of a revolutionary disposition," declared the council of San Felipe in 1834, asking Austin's release from his Mexican prison.

CHAPTER 7

THE BREAKING POINT

Texas was drifting inexorably toward revolution although her leaders were reluctant to recognize—or admit—it. The federal system, which held some hope for Texan home rule, was dead. A thorough dictatorship ignoring the will of the people was governing all Mexico—except Texas—by military force. The Mexican part of Coahuila y Texas was torn by a civil war in which Texans took no part and had little interest.

Customs collectors were again harassing the Texans—and Texans were again bedeviling the collectors. General Cos was marching more and more troops into Texas—not pitiful conscripts like earlier garrisons but soldiers trained by war-seasoned veterans. But bellicose Texans, even impetuous William B. Travis, who twice had defied the military and normally was ready for any fight, advised the Texans they had "better be quiet and settle down for a while." Austin, the one man Texans would follow in a crisis, was still detained in Mexico City.

Quietly committees of safety and correspondence set to work passing news—and rumors—from one community to another, and orators were denouncing dictatorship and governmental incompetence just as their grandfathers had done in 1775–76. One after another, Texas mass meetings demanded a general consultation "to secure peace if it is to be obtained on constitutional terms, and to prepare for war—if war be inevitable."

Three weeks before the election of delegates to the Consultation, a disillusioned Stephen F. Austin at long last landed in Texas from a vessel that fought off an armed Mexican ship at the mouth of the Brazos. A Texan reported that they all were of one mind: "if Colonel Austin is for peace, we are for peace; if he is for war, we are for war."

Seven days and nights Austin pondered. War could decimate his people and destroy all they had and all they hoped for. Submission could mean the end of human and property rights that Texans believed inalienable. He saw no middle ground. "War is our only recourse," he solemnly announced September 8, and urged election of the wisest Texans to the Consultation.

Before the Consultation could meet, before even delegates could be chosen, the Texans were at war.

Citizens of Gonzales routed a detachment of soldiers who had come from San Antonio to fetch back a government cannon which had been there for years, protecting colonists against Indians. The commandant needed it now to protect Mexicans against the colonists. The Texans loaded the old gun with scrap iron, hoisted a "Come and Take It" flag, and fired. That was October 2, 1835.

Alarmed colonists flocked to the scene, 300 of them, and organized the Army of the People. They furnished their own arms, elected their officers and a board of twelve volunteers "to advise with and direct" the commander. They named Austin their general and straggled toward San Antonio, their number doubling, their sense of invincibility skyrocketing after every skirmish with the enemy.

As they camped near the Mexican stronghold, the Consultation got under way at San Felipe November 3—Austin's birthday. Fifteen delegates demanded a no-nonsense declaration of independence; but Sam Houston—a resident for six months—and thirty-two others thought it more prudent to say Texans were loyal Mexican citizens fighting to restore the federal Constitution of 1824. They created a State of Texas in the federal union that Santa Anna had dissolved, and elected Houston commander of a nonexistent regular army but not of the men already in the field.

FREEMEN OF TEXAS

To Arms!!! To Arms!!!!

"Now 's the day, & now 's the hour."

Camp of the Volunteers,
Friday Night, 11 o'clock;
October 2, 1835.

Fellow Citizens:—

We have prevailed on our fellow citizen Wm. H. Wharton, Esq. to return and communicate to you the following express, and also to urge as many as can by possibility leave their homes to repair to Gonzales immediately, "armed and equipped for war even to the knife." On the receipt of this intelligence the Volunteers immediately resolved to march to Gonzales to aid their countrymen. We are just now starting which must apologize for the brevity of this communication. We refer you to Mr. Wharton for an explanation of our wishes, opinions and intentions, and also for such political information as has come into our hands. If Texas will now act promptly; she will soon be redeemed from that worse than Egyptian bondage which now cramps her resources and retards her prosperity.

David Randon,
Wm. J. Bryand,
J. W. Fannin, Jr.
F. T. Wells,
Geo. Sutherland,
B. T. Archer,
W. D. C. Hall,
W. H. Jack,
Wm. T. Austin,
P. D. McNeel.

P. S. An action took place on yesterday at Gonzales, in which the Mexican Commander and several soldiers were slain—no loss on the American side

Cos with his 1,200 soldiers was entrenched in San Antonio. The volunteers in the Army of the People kept up a loose siege until cold weather came, then prepared to withdraw. They paused when a grizzled man who had been a filibuster, a Mexican officer, a Texas empresario, and recently a guest in General Cos's *calabozo,* shouted:

"Who will go with old Ben Milam into San Antonio?"

Three hundred volunteered, and while Cos's men fired from roofs, Milam's Texans "went through the old adobe and picket houses of the Mexicans, using battering rams made out of logs ten or twelve feet long. . . . How the women and children would yell," one remembered. Cos herded his soldiers into the Alamo and on December 11 surrendered, promising to march below the Rio Grande and never return to Texas. Cos lost 150 killed; four Texans died—one of them Milam.

Ben Milam.

Veramendi Palace where Milam died.

By Christmas there was not a Mexican soldier on Texan soil and the Army of the People practically evaporated. Incredibly a handful of farmers had defied the dictator of seven million Mexicans and evicted all his soldiers.

In their isolated homes the Texans heard little of what had happened at San Antonio—or what was going on at San Felipe, capital of their improvised state. They seemed not to suspect that Santa Anna would move against Texas as he had against Zacatecas and Coahuila and every other region that challenged his dictatorship. Apathy was the mood of most Texans that winter. But among leaders of the Army of the People and in the makeshift government there was frenzied activity—all of it at cross-purposes and all of it futile.

At San Felipe Governor Henry Smith and his executive council attended to business for a while, then began examining the patriotism and character of each other. By January, 1836, the Governor was shouting: "I am tired of watching scoundrels abroad and scoundrels at home. . . . [This] caucussing, intriguing, corrupt council . . . will stand adjourned until the first of March. . . ."

The Council pronounced the Governor "vulgar and depraved, and his present disposition that of a disorganizer and a tyrant" and deposed him. Smith refused to give up, but the Council named a new governor. For two crucial months Texas had two governments, countermanding each other's orders and keeping the printer busy with vitriolic proclamations and broadsides.

The military situation was hopeless. Houston, commander in chief of the Regular Army, had officers for 26 companies but no privates; he had no authority over the Volunteers. Nor did the provisional government control these men who had been in the field for months and were daily being joined by new arrivals from the States. After the Volunteer commanders refused even to listen to Houston's advice, he gave up and went among the Indians in East Texas to make peace treaties with them. If white men would not listen to him, his red brothers did. They promised to be good and they kept their promise.

At Goliad James W. Fannin, an imaginative twenty-seven-year-old Georgian, assembled the largest force in Texas, about five hundred men fresh from the States. He had been a West Point cadet and was not disposed to take orders, even advice, from a mere militiaman like Houston. He regarded himself as commander in chief.

At San Patricio Frank W. Johnson was signing himself "Commander in Chief of the Federal Volunteer Army of Texas" as he rounded up men and horses to join Fannin in carrying the war into Mexico by way of Matamoros. He had taken all movable supplies—and 200 men—from the Alamo over the protest of the commander there.

Some commanders reported to Governor Smith, others to the Council; but none received firm direction from any governmental source. Each worked out his own plans in ignorance of what the others were doing. Texas neither abandoned nor provisioned her isolated frontier outposts.

San Antonio had been garrisoned, after a fashion, since December when Cos surrendered it. Residents of the town were bewildered, distrustful of both Texans and Mexicans. The Army of the People had drifted away—old settlers to their homes, newcomers toward the Rio Grande to join Fannin and Johnson. When the garrison dwindled to 104 dispirited and destitute men, Houston sent James Bowie with a squad to remove the men and equipment to Goliad and blow up the Alamo. Bowie came; but he soon resolved he would "rather die in these ditches than give them up to the enemy."

At the same time Governor Smith ordered William B. Travis, a colonel of the Regulars, to enlist 100 men to help hold the place. But Travis had only 30 recruits to show for two weeks' desperate recruiting. He found the "people are cold and indifferent; they have lost confidence in their own government and officers. . . . Volunteers can no longer be had or relied upon." He led his men to San Antonio and assumed command of the garrison. But most of the men were Volunteers and they elected Bowie commander. Each commander considered himself in complete charge. Finally they sensibly but reluctantly agreed on joint responsibility.

In the name of the People of Texas Sovereign and free—
To whom these presents shall come, Be it known.

That I, Henry Smith, Governor ~~of the people~~ of Texas ~~sovereign and free~~, by virtue of the authority vested in me as Governor aforesaid, do hereby ~~authorise and appoint Commiss~~ John Forbes, Sam Houston and John Cameron Esqs as Commissioners on the part of the Government of Texas, in conformity with the Declaration of the chosen delegates of all Texas in Convention assembled in the month of November last, setting forth the external bounds within which certain Indians therein named are to be settled. And in conformity with an Ordinance and Decree passed by the Legislative Council of Texas under date of the 22d inst authorising the appointment of the said Houston, Forbes and Cameron for the purposes aforesaid to treat with the said Indian tribes in conformity with the superior declaration of the Convention, and pursuant to and in conformity with the said Ordinance and decree as above designated, and to be governed by the accompanying instructions ~~All acts performed by the said~~ Commissioners on the part and in the name of the People of Texas, within the purview and by virtue of this authority shall be valid and ultimately ratified by this Government, in good faith, ~~when~~ finally ratified or ~~sanctioned by this~~ Government.

In testimony of which I Henry Smith Governor as aforesaid have hereunto set my hand and affixed my private seal, no seal of office being yet provided.

Done and signed at my office in the Town of San Felipe, this 28th day of December Eighteen hundred and thirty five

Nine words stricken null
Line added good

Henry Smith

Governor

Chas. B. Stewart

Secretary of Executive

That was the situation as Santa Anna was moving his 6,000 troops and his best generals into Texas, vowing to punish the "perfidy, ingratitude, and the restless spirit of the colonists" in a single scorched-earth campaign. As they marched inland, the Texans offered no resistance.

February 23 Santa Anna's troops converged on San Antonio. Travis had written ten days earlier: "We are illy prepared . . . we have not more than 150 men here and they in a very disorganized state. . . . For Gods sake, and the sake of our country, send us reinforcements . . . I am determined to defend it to the last, and should Bejar fall, your friend will be buried beneath its ruins."

Jim Bowie, a Texan since 1828, was in almost every skirmish against Mexico until his death in the Alamo, although his wife was Mexican.

Spanish Franciscans built the Alamo as Mission San Antonio de Valero in 1724 and worked there almost a century. This sketch by Colonel José Juan Sanchez Estrada, made in 1829, shows the façade of the chapel that was destroyed in the 1836 siege.

four thousand in four or five days.
If this call is neglected, I am determined to sustain myself as long as
possible & die like a soldier
who never forgets what is due to
his own honor & that of his
country —

Victory or Death.

William Barret Travis
Lt. Col. comdt.

P S The Lord is on our side —
When the enemy appeared in sight
we had not three bushels of corn —
We have since found in deserted
houses 80 or 90 bushels & got into
the walls 20 or 30 head of Beeves —

Travis

February 24, as Santa Anna closed in on the Alamo, Travis sent through the lines the most heroic letter in American history. Addressed "To the People of Texas and All Americans in the world," it promised "I shall never surrender or retreat. . . . *Victory or death!"*

David Crockett and his Tennessee boys had arrived and his drolleries and his fiddle were infusing new spirit in the recalcitrant Texans, who withdrew into the three-acre enclosure of the ancient mission San Antonio de Valero, now called the Alamo. Protected by the mission walls, three feet thick and nine to twelve feet high, the Texans prepared for siege. From homes vacated as Santa Anna neared they gathered rations to last a month. They mounted their cannon on earthen mounds and scaffolds, cleaned their guns, and whetted their bowie knives. Bowie, fatally ill with tuberculosis, fell from a scaffold the first day of siege, crushing his ribs, and he soon developed pneumonia. That solved the problem of command. Travis took the whole responsibility. In the face of the enemy, discord evaporated and the strangely assorted group of men became united in determination.

David Crockett was already a legend in the United States before he came to Texas in 1836 "to fight for his rights" and died in the Alamo, aged fifty. A backwoods Tennessean, he served as a magistrate, militia colonel, state legislator, and United States Congressman before his refusal to be a "gee-woa-haw" follower of Andrew Jackson ended his political career there. He told his constituents after his defeat for Congress, "As for you, you can go to hell; I'm agoin' to Texas." His first letter from Texas said, "I would rather be in my present situation [en route to the Alamo] than to be elected to a seat in Congress for life." His backwoods humor, his fiddling, and his marksmanship enlivened the spirits of the men in the Alamo, and he probably killed more Mexicans than any of the other defenders of the fortress. The circumstances of his death would have made him a legend if he had not already been one—and more than a century later the Crockett legend is still growing. He was not illiterate—he wrote several books—but he epitomized the down to earthiness of the American frontiersman. He was a Texan barely two months, but his name is inseparably linked with the epic of the state.

Contemporary English cartoon of David Crockett

'HELLO, FRIEND, DON'T FORGET THAT VOTE.'

DAVID CROCKETT
I am happy to acknowledge this to be
the only correct likeness that has been
taken of me. David Crockett

Santa Anna was in no hurry to make the assault, once he had the Texans penned in the old mission. He ordered grenades and grape and canister thrown into the Alamo, more to harass the Texans than to kill them. Travis reported on March 3: "At least two hundred shells have fallen inside our works without having injured a single man . . . and we have killed many of the enemy." The 32 men of Gonzales, with their "Come and Take It" flag, had managed to get through the Mexican lines to join Travis.

Fannin at Goliad had been ordered to San Antonio. He vacillated, started, then turned back. It was too late to march to Matamoros, too late to reinforce Travis, too late to do anything effective. He and his men, isolated, awaited destruction.

When all hope of reinforcements was gone, Travis offered his 182 men what Dobie calls a choice between life and immortality. Only one left.

At last before dawn on March 6, in freezing weather, the Mexicans sounded the *deguello* (no quarter), and closed in with scaling ladders, axes, crowbars, and spikes. The Texans manned their cannon, and sharpshooters fired from the top of the walls; but although they killed hundreds of the enemy they could not prevent their breaching the wall. Through the breach the Mexicans poured, to kill and be killed in hand-to-hand combat until the last Texan lay dead. Travis died across his cannon carriage, a single bullet through his head; Crockett died surrounded by 16 Mexican corpses, his knife up to the hilt in the chest

of one of them; Bowie, broken and delirious, died on his cot in the chapel, surrounded by dead Mexicans. The only survivors of the siege were noncombatants—five or six women, a few children, and two Negro slaves.

Santa Anna sent the Texans' flag to Mexico City with the report that he "lost about 70 killed and 300 wounded" and had counted 600 Texan corpses. His secretary, with an eye to fact rather than propaganda, said: "We brought to San Antonio more than five thousand men and we lost during the siege 1,544 of the best of them. The Texans fought more like devils than men." It was unquestionably a complete Mexican victory; but as one of his officers told Santa Anna, "another such victory would ruin them."

During the slaughter at the Alamo, another handful of Texans met one hundred and fifty miles to the east, at Washington-on-the-Brazos—"a rare place to hold a national convention in . . . not one decent house . . . [its only street] an opening cut out of the woods, the stumps still standing." In an unfinished shed, temperature near freezing, they set about their work of freedom. To preside they elected Richard Ellis of Red River whose constituents, uncertain whether they lived in Arkansas or Texas, had elected him to represent them in both places.

Lorenzo de Zavala, distinguished fugitive from Santa Anna, began a keynote address: "Mr. President, an eminent Roman statesman once said . . ." but Thomas J. Rusk's burst of realism stopped it: "It behooves the Convention to give less thought to dead Romans and more attention to live Mexicans!" Thereafter for sixteen days the delegates followed Rusk's advice.

Next day, March 2, George C. Childress, who had arrived from Tennessee just three weeks before he was elected a delegate, was ready with a Declaration of Independence that argued the Texan cause as eloquently as the oldest colonist could have done. It was unanimously adopted, without debate.

Sam Houston, whose constituency amounted to 44 Irishmen from Refugio among whom he had spent one day, signed the Declaration on his forty-second birthday and four days later departed as commander of all military forces of the new Republic. Hurriedly the delegates put together a Constitution, created an ad-interim government headed by David G. Burnet and Lorenzo de Zavala, and rushed homeward. They knew the Alamo had fallen and nothing stood between them and Santa Anna's wrath.

Washington-on-the-Brazos, where independence was declared.

Lorenzo de Zavala.

Thomas J. Rusk.

FRIENDS

AND

CITIZENS OF TEXAS

Information, of a character not to be questioned, has just been received from Col. Fannin, which states that Santa Ana, at the head of four thousand men, has crossed the San Antonio river, leaving Goliad in his rear, and is moving upon our public stores, and thence to Gonsales. Ths force is independent of the army under Siezma before Bejar A general turn out has commenced and is going on here and westward, and as far as known. Citizens in every part of the country, it is hoped, will be no less ready to defend their homes, their wives, and children.

We advise that every armed vessel which can be had should be despatched at once, to scour the Gulf, and all points where most likely to interespt the stores and supplies of the enemy, and every precaution adopted for protecting our own stores.

JOHN R. JONES, } *Standing*
THOMAS GAY, } *Committee.*

San Felipe, March 2, 1836.

George C. Childress, Tennessee lawyer-editor, drafted the Texas Declaration of Independence which was unanimously adopted March 2, 1836.

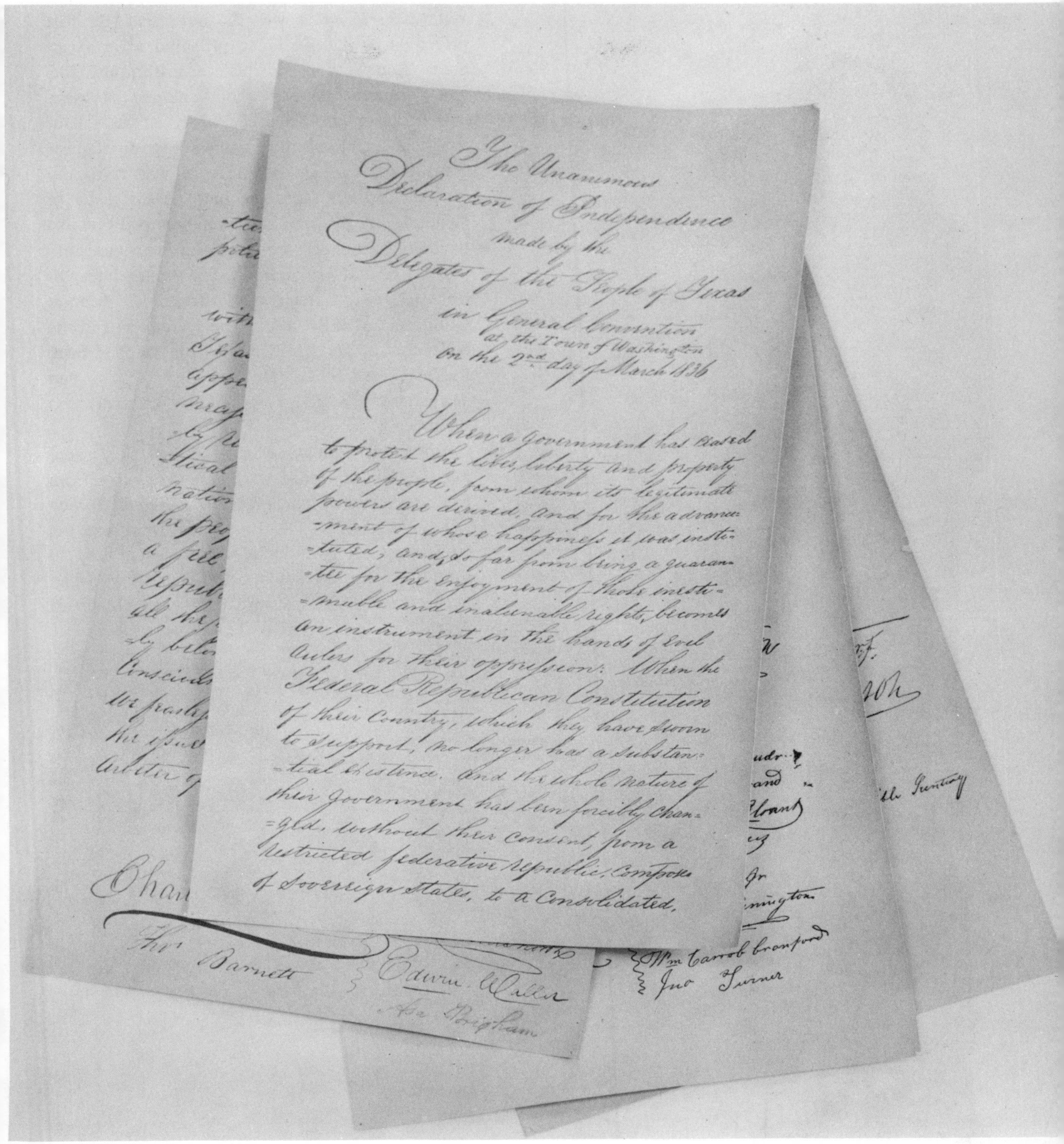

The Unanimous
Declaration of Independence
made by the
Delegates of the People of Texas
in General Convention
at the Town of Washington
on the 2nd day of March 1836

When a Government has ceased to protect the lives, liberty and property of the people, from whom its legitimate powers are derived, and for the advancement of whose happiness it was instituted, and so far from being a guarantee for the enjoyment of those inestimable and inalienable rights, becomes an instrument in the hands of evil rulers for their oppression: When the Federal Republican Constitution of their Country, which they have sworn to support, no longer has a substantial existence, and the whole nature of their Government has been forcibly changed, without their consent, from a restricted federative republic, composed of sovereign states, to a consolidated,

Thos Barnett
Edwin Waller
Asa Brigham
Wm Carroll Crawford
Jno Turner

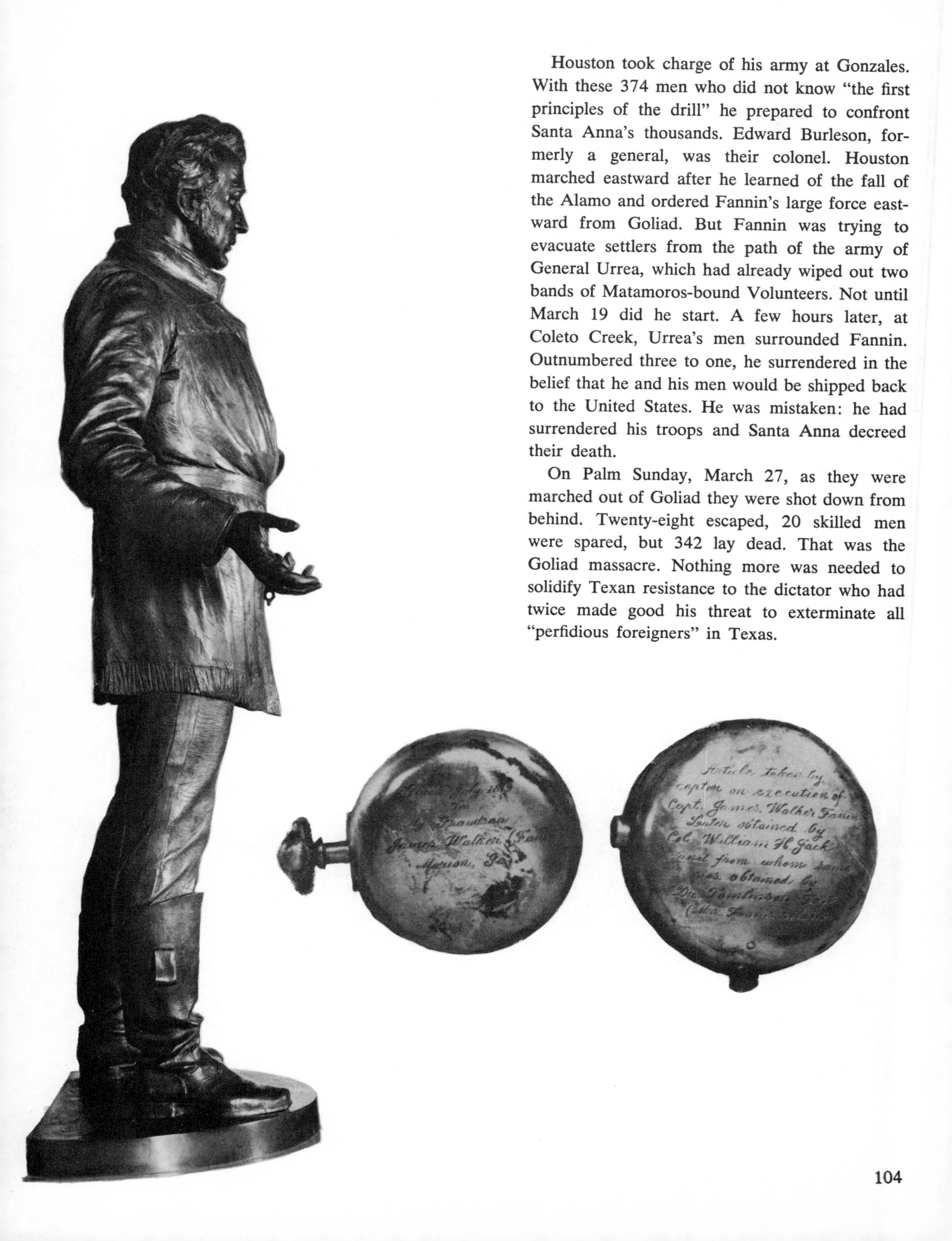

Houston took charge of his army at Gonzales. With these 374 men who did not know "the first principles of the drill" he prepared to confront Santa Anna's thousands. Edward Burleson, formerly a general, was their colonel. Houston marched eastward after he learned of the fall of the Alamo and ordered Fannin's large force eastward from Goliad. But Fannin was trying to evacuate settlers from the path of the army of General Urrea, which had already wiped out two bands of Matamoros-bound Volunteers. Not until March 19 did he start. A few hours later, at Coleto Creek, Urrea's men surrounded Fannin. Outnumbered three to one, he surrendered in the belief that he and his men would be shipped back to the United States. He was mistaken: he had surrendered his troops and Santa Anna decreed their death.

On Palm Sunday, March 27, as they were marched out of Goliad they were shot down from behind. Twenty-eight escaped, 20 skilled men were spared, but 342 lay dead. That was the Goliad massacre. Nothing more was needed to solidify Texan resistance to the dictator who had twice made good his threat to exterminate all "perfidious foreigners" in Texas.

The government had fled on horseback toward the coast; Houston reportedly was moving his army to the United States border, and colonists were rushing pell-mell toward the Sabine, leaving everything behind them. The confused mass movement that ended April 21 is known as the Runaway Scrape. The Republic of Texas seemed about to die aborning.

When Fannin surrendered, he and his men believed they would be shipped back to the United States, but actually they placed themselves "at the disposal of the Supreme Mexican Government" which had already decreed death to all foreigners taken in arms. Urrea, to whom they surrendered, begged clemency, but Santa Anna ordered their execution. Fannin begged to be shot through the heart and that his watch be sent to his family. His face was riddled by bullets, but his watch was saved. The few survivors of the massacre gratefully remembered Señora Francisca Álvarez, wife of a Mexican officer, who cared for the wounded and dying, and helped some to escape. She was the Angel of Goliad. Goliad was originally known as La Bahía (pronounced Labadie by Texans), but it was renamed Goliad by the legislature of Coahuila y Texas in 1829, an anagram of Hidalgo, father of Mexican independence. Mexicans at San Jacinto, a month after the massacre, heard the Texans' battle cry: "Remember the Alamo! Remember Goliad!"

Goliad cannon

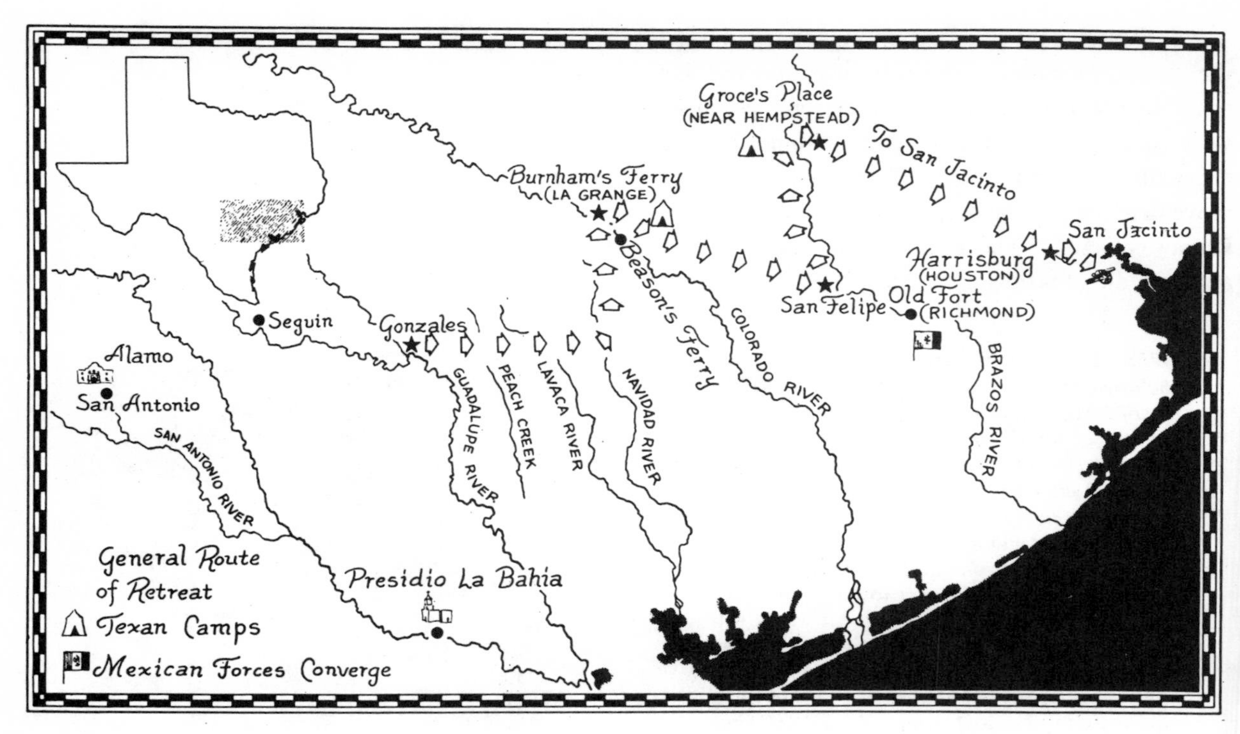

Arrows indicate the route followed by the Texan army from March 14, when Gonzales was evacuated, to April 20, when it halted at San Jacinto. Erastus (Deaf) Smith, famous scout, burned Vince's bridge before the battle.

Santa Anna's armies deployed leisurely through the settlements, living off the country, burning towns, spreading panic, meeting no resistance. Houston enigmatically moved eastward and southward against orders of the President and his secretary of war; but at least he managed to keep out of the enemy's range and to thwart recurrent soldier plots to depose him. "I consulted none—held no councils of war," he said. "If I err, the blame is mine."

After burning Harrisburg on Buffalo Bayou, Santa Anna moved up to the Plain of San Jacinto. There he camped to await reinforcements that increased his force to 1,265 men. The Texan army, learning of this, pitched camp less than a mile from Santa Anna's on April 20. At long last Houston and his men were face to face with the enemy, and they dined on food from a captured Mexican supply ship.

That afternoon a few shots were exchanged but neither Santa Anna nor Houston was yet ready for battle. As they waited, General Cos arrived with reinforcements for Santa Anna and the Texans cut down Vince's bridge over which they had marched—and might have retreated.

Sam Houston at San Jacinto.

The only Texan flag at San Jacinto was this silk banner made by ladies in Kentucky and brought to Texas by Sidney Sherman's volunteers before independence was declared. It is now in the State Capitol at Austin.

The Texans were impatient to attack next morning, but Houston withheld his order until about three-thirty in the afternoon. Then, screened by trees and rising ground, 910 bearded and ragged Texans crept silently and tensely toward the Mexican breastworks, where all was silent. It was siesta time. A Texan fifer struck up "Will You Come to the Bower," then the men, shouting "Remember the Alamo! Remember Goliad!" burst into the Mexican camp and seized the artillery. They emptied their pistols and bashed skulls with gun butts, deaf to pleas of "Me no Alamo! Me no Goliad!"

Will You Come to the Bower?

Above, *Mexican flag thought to have been taken from Santa Anna's headquarters at San Jacinto. Santa Anna's spurs presented to General Houston after the battle.* Left, *San Jacinto battlefield, showing location of the armies in relation to the Monument.*

The Battle of San Jacinto.

In eighteen minutes the battle became a foot-race which ended at dark. The Plain of San Jacinto was littered with bodies of men and horses and the bayou tinged with blood. Santa Anna did not participate. Awakened from siesta by gunfire, he "became aware that we were being attacked"—and decamped in disguise. But the Texans captured him in flight, took 730 of his men, all his supplies and matériel, and counted 630 Mexicans dead, 208 wounded. Only nine of the Texans died; only 20—including Houston—were wounded.

That San Jacinto is one of the decisive battles of the world is part of the Texan creed. Whatever military experts may say of its technical flaws, it determined the immediate course of Texas and the ultimate course of United States history.

It transferred Texas from Latin America to Anglo-America. Heirs of Cortes and Montezuma left indelible marks there but the future belonged to the race of men the empresarios brought in.

Santa Anna, looking more like a laborer than a Dictator and Generalissimo, stood captive before General Houston after the battle saying: "You can afford to be generous, you who have captured the Napoleon of the West." The Texan soldiers wanted to hang him to the nearest tree (note the coiled rope in Edward Burleson's hand), but Houston saved his life and handed him over to the Government. Eventually Santa Anna returned to Mexico, became president again, and again harassed the Texans from the remote safety of Mexico City.

Before and after the war for Independence, General Houston was courting Miss Anna Raguet, beautiful daughter of a prominent Nacogdoches family. While a surgeon dressed his wounds after his victory at San Jacinto, he sent an orderly to gather magnolia leaves and sent them to Miss Anna with a note: "These are the laurels I send you from the battle field of San Jacinto. Thine. Houston." The General had won the battle but he lost the girl; she married Dr. Robert A. Irion, Houston's closest friend. It was four days after the battle when he finished his official report to the Government. "The conflict," he wrote, "lasted about eighteen minutes. . . . The rout commenced at half-past four, and the pursuit by the main army continued until nightfall. . . . For the commanding general to attempt discrimination as to the conduct of those who commanded in the action, or those who were commanded, would be impossible. Our success in the action is conclusive proof of their daring intrepidity and courage. . . ." He sent copies of the Report to newspapers in the United States. This one, addressed to the Louisiana Advertiser, *is the only known draft of the Report signed by Houston.*

The tallest monument in Texas (and in the United States) is San Jacinto Memorial at the battlefield. It rises 570 feet with a museum area 125 feet square at its base and a 34-foot Texas star at its apex. On eight massive exterior panels are engraved the salient facts of Texas history, and above the panels a frieze depicts the Anglo-American colonization of Texas. The Museum's permanent exhibits highlight the story of the region from the time of Cortes to the War Between the States, with special emphasis on the Spanish, Mexican, and Anglo-American colonization. In the collections are half a million pages of documents, a rich reference library, as well as thousands of relics and pictures.

CHAPTER 8

TALENTED AMATEURS

The Texas Republic, born in a gunshop and certified on a single battlefield, claimed more land than the original thirteen states then had—379,054 square miles, 338,332 of them unsurveyed and uninhabited. With almost absurd confidence its 30,000 men, women, and children—one for each 80,000 acres—created a nation that had every essential attribute but one. It had a president punctiliously addressed as Excellency, congressmen, senators, cabinet officers, diplomatic corps, army, navy, rangers, customs officers, postmasters, and a horde of civil servants. The only thing it lacked was solvency.

Texan paper currency and bonds were handsomely engraved and the government tried to keep them negotiable—"taxing, borrowing, begging, selling . . . robbing and cheating," a financier said—but currency depreciated 90 per cent and the deficit grew from one to twelve millions in ten years. The error, Anson Jones thought, was "thinking and acting as a great nation when we were but a first-rate *county*"; but not many shared that view. Texans of 1836 were expansive. They believed that what their Republic lacked, Providence—and they—would provide. "I know not on earth, and never have heard of, a community so small, so well able to take care of itself," was a Tennesseean's verdict on Texas in the summer of 1836.

Most Texans thought annexation only a matter of months, but others expected their Republic to endure forever, expanding west to the Pacific, southward into Mexico, and maybe eastward through the slave states to the Atlantic, to outstrip the United States.

The malleability of Texas destiny made politics the vocation of many and the avocation of the rest. There were experienced politicians among them and the country "was absolutely overrun," Houston said, with "noisy, second-rate" advocates of "rash and extreme measures." The small population and the number of offices made every man a potential statesman.

Every summer all congressmen, a third of the senators, and some local officials had to be elected; every third year a president. There were issues enough, but candidates and voters preferred discussion of personalities. The winner normally was the man who proved his opponent a greater rascal than he, while declaring his own faith in, or loathing for, Sam Houston—even when the Old Hero was not in the race. There were no parties, no platforms; only friends of Houston and enemies of Houston, who switched allegiance unpredictably.

Houston's admirers swept him into the presidency in the first national election with 5,119 votes out of 6,641. For the vice presidency nobody ran against Mirabeau Buonaparte Lamar, a poetic Georgia editor who had landed in Texas in April, sword in hand, and inquired the way to the battlefield. Private, cavalry colonel, and a hero of San Jacinto, secretary of war, major general, vice president—all in six months. Texas was generous to Lamar in 1836.

At the end of the year of revolution the Republic of Texas was a going concern—so far as documents and constitutional officials could make her—but she had, and created, more problems than she could solve in ten years.

Santa Anna had to be disposed of. Soldiers wanted, and tried, to hang him. Congress thought he had value as a hostage. President Houston, the realist, overriding everybody's advice, released him to "keep Mexico in commotion for years." That made neither Texans nor Mexicans happy; only Santa Anna.

The army had to be controlled or disbanded. After San Jacinto it grew to about twenty-five hundred men, mostly newcomers, bent on war and defying the government. When Major General Lamar arrived in camp, the men voted 1,500 to 179 to reject him; they wanted Felix (Long Shanks) Huston, one of their own men. Next Brigadier General Albert Sidney Johnston appeared. Huston disabled him in a duel, retained command, then tried to get Congress to let him invade Mexico. While he was busy lobbying, the President quietly furloughed all but a few scattered companies and Long Shanks quit the army—and Texas—in disgust.

After 1837 Texas had no army problem—and few soldiers. Rangers and, in emergencies, militia and short-term volunteers, stood between the Texans and all their enemies on land. Maritime defense was another matter. Before independence Texas commissioned privateers and bought four little ships for a navy that kept the coast clear during the war. But the navy had no part in the famous exploit on water two months after San Jacinto, when Major I. W. Burton's mounted Rangers captured three Mexican vessels and supplies worth $25,000 at Copano. Burton's men were the original Horse Marines.

Ship by ship the navy disappeared during 1837. The *Independence,* bringing Minister W. H. Wharton home from Washington with news of recognition of independence, was captured by a Mexican ship named, appropriately, *Vencedor del Alamo.* Wharton went to jail in Matamoros; the ship was added to the Mexican navy. The sea swallowed two brave ships—the *Invincible* and the *Brutus*—and the *Liberty* was sold in New Orleans for repair charges which the Republic couldn't pay. When Houston's term ended, the secretary of the navy controlled only a navy yard at Galveston, although eight new ships were on order.

Major Burton's Horse Marines.

HISTORY

OF THE

CAPTIVITY AND PROVIDENTIAL RELEASE THERE-FROM OF

MRS. CAROLINE HARRIS,

Wife of the late Mr. Richard Harris, of Franklin Co., State of N. York; who, with Mrs Clarissa Plummer, wife of Mr. James Plummer, were, in the Spring of 1835, (with their unfortunate husbands,) taken prisoners by the Camanche tribe of Indians, while emigrating from said Franklin Co (N. Y.) to Texas; and after having been made to witness the tragical deaths of their husbands, and held nearly two years in bondage, were providentially redeemed therefrom by two of their countrymen attached to a company of Santa Fe Fur Traders.

It was the misfortune of Mrs. Harris, & her unfortunate female companion (soon after the deaths of their husbands,) to be separated by, and compelled to become the companions of, and to cohabit with, two disgusting Indian Chiefs, and from whom they received the most cruel and beastly treatment.

Indians had to be coped with. There were about fifteen thousand of them: Cherokees and various semi-civilized tribes near the Sabine who wanted only to be left alone on the land they thought was theirs; in the west, Comanches and other savage nomads—buffalo hunters, raiders, scalpers, and horse thieves; and in between docile tribes that plotted seldom but sometimes joined the red men against the whites.

Houston, master of Indian psychology, dealt patiently and firmly with all of them. The Cherokees had been promised their land by every government Texas had had, but Congress refused to grant it. Personal friendship between the President and Chief The Bowl insured Cherokee neutrality during a Mexican-inspired Indian rebellion in 1838, which 600 Texan volunteers quelled; but the Cherokees were restive and apprehensive. On the western frontier Houston stationed Rangers to watch the Comanches, who made only occasional raids. His policy was inexpensive and his status as a sort of honorary Indian made it successful. Most Texans thought it too soft.

Political news filled newspapers, but the real concerns of the Texans were getting land, farming, ranching, town building, speculation. About one hundred thousand people came to Texas while it was a republic, and everywhere between the Sabine and Fort Worth, Austin and San Antonio, there were new little towns and homesteads. Free or cheap land was plentiful and hard times in the States—panic from 1837 to 1842—made Texas as attractive as it had been in the 1820s. The Republic gave soldiers and families acreage ranging from a square mile to a mere half section. Latecomers bought at ten to fifty cents an acre or became squatters without formality. New empresarios brought immigrants from everywhere. More than ever before, Texas was a land of beginning again. It was the new Cotton Kingdom.

Executive Mansion of the Republic at Houston.

The J. M. Blue House at Independence is of stone and timber with broad porches.

Editor Charles de Morse lived in this house at Clarksville.

Beyond the basic one of utility, the houses of the Republic of Texas showed many influences. The Blue home at Independence, once the Athens of Texas, has a first story of stone, second story of timber, and a broad, two-story porch. Many of the plantation houses were similar in design. The sprawling DeMorse house at Clarksville is a frame cottage of a type common to towns, while the McIntyre house at Anderson is typical of the simple farm homes of the Republic. Note the picket fence, the well with its pulley, the watering trough made of a hollow log, the inevitable fig tree, left, *and the wild grapevine growing through the branches of the tree,* right.

French, Spanish, Mexican, and Anglo-American motifs are found in the houses citizens of the Republic built. The Toalson home at Independence is stone plastered over—a simple Mexican house with an Anglo-American front porch. The Freeman Inn at Navasota, an early stage stand, is a frame two-and-a-half story structure with an enclosed outside stairway and overhanging roof. General Thomas J. Chambers's home at Anahuac has an outside spiral stairway and a Texan star in the attic window.

TELEGRAPH.

EDITED BY FRANCIS MOORE, Jun.

Houston, Saturday, Jan. 13, 1838.

PHILOSOPHICAL SOCIETY OF TEXAS.

During the recent session of Congress a number of **gentlemen, from different parts of the republic,** formed themselves into an association under the above name, to be established at the seat of government, but to be purely scientific and literary in its character.

At a meeting on the 5th December, held at the capitol, a constitution was adopted, and the following gentlemen were elected officers:—

Mirabeau B. Lamar, *President,*
Ashbel Smith, 1*st*
Robert A. Irion, 2*d*
Anson Jones, 3*d*
Joseph Rowe, 4*th*
David S. Kaufman, 5*th* } *Vice Presidents.*
Wm. Fairfax Gray, *Recording Secretary,*
David G. Burnet, *Corresponding do.*
Augustus C. Allen, *Treasurer,*
John Birdsall, *Librarian.*

Subjects for investigation or discussion were assigned to the several members, and a memorial adopted to be presented to the Congress, asking a suitable endowment and encouragement for the institution. The following preamble to the constitution and extract from the memorial to Congress exhibit in a condensed view the scope proposed to be embraced by the society. Objects so important to the scientific enquirer generally, and calculated to add so largely to the national character and national wealth, it is confidently trusted will not only receive the fostering care and patronage of the legislature, but will attract the cordial co-operation of all the mental energy and literary acquirement of our infant republic.

Names of Members.—

Mirabeau B. Lamar
Ashbel Smith
Tho J Rusk
Wm. H. Wharton
Joseph Rowe
Angus McNeill
A. C. Allen
G. W. Bonnell
Joseph Baker
Patrick C Jack
W. Fairfax Gray
Jno. A. Wharton
D. S. Kaufman
[illegible]
Anson Jones
Littleton Fowler
A. C. Horton
J. W. Bunton
Edward T. Branch
Henry Smith
Hugh McLeod
T. Jefferson Chambers
Sam Houston
R. A. Irion

Texans had intellectual and social interests, too. In 1837 twenty-six men founded the Philosophical Society for the Collection and Diffusion of Knowledge; and formal balls on anniversary occasions, as well as the theater, gave the ladies an opportunity to dress in silks and satins.

INAUGURATION BALL.

The pleasure of your company is particul[arly] solicited at a Ball, to be given at the Capitol, Monday evening, the 13th inst.

Austin, 10th December, 1841.

MANAGERS.

JOHN A. GREER,	J. G. CHALMERS,
K. L. ANDERSON,	JOSEPH DANIELS,
JOHN D. MORRIS,	J. W. ROBERTSON,
SAM. WHITING,	JACOB SNIVELY,
W. L. CAZNEAU,	A. C. HYDE,
J. W. HARRISON,	J. F. JOHNSON,
JAMES B. SHAW,	G. H. HARRISON,
T. G. FORSTER,	CHARLES MASON,
ALEX. M'DONALD,	C. DE MORSE.

"Merrily every bosom boundeth,
Merrily, oh!
When the voice of Freedom soundeth,
Merrily, oh!"

The pleasure of your Company is respectfully solicited at a BALL to be given on Friday, the 2nd March, in the REPRESENTATIVE'S HALL.

MANAGERS.

A. JACKSON DAVIS,	JAMES W. [illegible]
P. W. HUMPHREYS,	WM. N. BRONAUGH,
F. R. LUBBOCK,	J. W. ELDREDGE,
H. P. BEE,	J. C. ELDREDGE.

SAN JACINTO BALL.

The pleasure of your company is requested at a Ball, to be given at FLOYD & COLLINS' HOTEL, on the Evening of the 20th inst. in honor of the Battle of San Jacinto.

MANAGERS.

[illegible] B. LAMAR,	GEN. T. J. RUSK,
[illegible]STON,	J. TEMPLE DOSWELL,
[illegible]ZAVALA,	E. FLOYD,
	P. HALPIN,
[illegible] ALLEN.	J. W. CRUGER,

[illegible] 1838.

THEATRE.

The Public are respectfully informed that the Scenery, which was materially injured in the voyage from the United States, having been repaired by Messrs. Chambers & Jackson, the Company will have the honor of making their appearance on

Monday Evening, June 11, 1838;

When will be presented Sheridan Knowles' celebrated Comedy of

THE

Hunchback.

MASTER WALTER	MR BARKER
SIR THOMAS CLIFFORD	CORRI
LORD TINSEL	JACKSON
MASTER WILFORD	ORMOND
MODUS	SARGENT
FATHOM	NEWTON
MASTER HEARTWELL	CHAMBERS
STEPHEN	HORN
JULIA	MRS. BARKER
HELEN	HUBBARD

Previous to the Comedy, Mr CARLOS will recite

AN OPENING ADDRESS.

After which the whole Company will sing

A New National Texian Anthem,

Written expressly for the occasion by Mr CORRI

THE WHOLE TO CONCLUDE WITH THE POPULAR FARCE OF

DUMB BELLE,

OR

I'm Perfection.

MR. MANVERS,	MR JACKSON
VIVIAN	CORRI
O'SMIRK	NEWTON
JAMES	CHAMBERS
ELIZA, (The Dumb Belle,)	MRS. BARKER
MARY	MISS VOGT

The members of the Orchestra having not yet arrived from Mobile, the Managers request the kind indulgence of their patrons for a few days.

Doors open at 7 1-2 o'clock. Performance to commence at 8 precisely.

[illegible] for seats either for the season or by the night, to be made [illegible] between the hours of 10 A. M. and 1 P. M. and from 4 [illegible] P. M. [illegible]

ANTI-TEXAS MEETING

AT FANEUIL HALL!

Friends of Freedom!

A proposition has been made, and will soon come up for consideration in the United States Senate, to annex Texas to the Union. This territory has been wrested from Mexico by violence and fraud. Such is the character of the leaders in this enterprise that the country has been aptly termed "that valley of rascals." It is large enough to make *nine* or *ten* States as large as Massachusetts. It was, under Mexico, a free territory. The freebooters have made it a slave territory. The design is to annex it, with its load of infamy and oppression, to the Union. The immediate result may be a war with Mexico—the ultimate result *will be* some 18 or 20 more slaveholders in the Senate of the United States, a still larger number in the House of Representatives, and the balance of power in the hands of the South! And if, when in a minority in Congress, slaveholders browbeat the North, demand the passage of gag laws, trample on the Right of Petition, and threaten, in defiance of the General Government, to hang every man, caught at the South, who dares to speak against their "domestic institutions," what limits shall be set to their intolerant demands and high handed usurpations, when they are in the majority?

All opposed to this scheme, of whatever sect or party, are invited to attend the meeting at the Old Cradle of Liberty, to-morrow, (Thursday Jan. 25,) at 10 o'clock, A. M., at which time addresses are expected from several able speakers.

Bostonians! Friends of Freedom!! Let your voices be heard in loud remonstrance against this scheme, fraught with such ruin to yourselves and such infamy to your country.

January 24, 1838.

Externally what Texas needed was recognition as an independent nation. Santa Anna, while a prisoner, agreed that Texas was independent, but Mexico promptly disavowed it. Houston's patron saint, Jackson, was President of the United States and Texans believed that Old Hickory would promptly recognize and annex Texas. But his term was expiring and he delayed even recognition until his last day in the White House. Van Buren, his successor, didn't want another slave state, which would split his party north and south. He declined flatly the Texan offer of annexation.

Then Texas sought friends in Europe. England wanted a share in the economic potential of Texas but her government opposed slavery. France agreed to send a commissioner to Texas and to consider recognition. In foreign affairs, Texas hoped much but accomplished little for three years.

...ième jour du mois de
...tembre de l'an de grace mil
...t cent trente neuf

twenty fifth day of September
in the year of Our Lord One
thousand eight hundred and thirty nine.

(LS) - Mal Duc de Dalmatie
(LS) - J Pinckney Henderson

Nous, ayant agréable le susdit Traité en
toutes et chacune des dispositions qui y sont
contenues, ainsi que les articles additionnels qui
le suivent, Déclarons, tant pour Nous que
pour nos héritiers et successeurs, qu'ils sont
approuvés, acceptés, ratifiés et confirmés et par ces
présentes signées de notre main, Nous les approuvons
acceptons, ratifions et confirmons Promettant en
foi et parole de Roi de les observer et de les
faire observer inviolablement sans jamais y contrevenir
ni permettre qu'il y soit contrevenu directement ni
indirectement pour quelque cause et sous quelque
prétexte que ce soit. En foi de quoi, Nous avons fait
mettre notre sceau à ces présentes Donné en notre
Palais de Fontainebleau, le deuxième jour du mois
d'Octobre de l'an de grâce mil huit cent trente neuf

Louis Philippe

Par le Roi

Mal Duc de Dalmatie

of all which We have caused the Great Seal of Our United Kingdom of Great
Britain and Ireland to be affixed to these Presents, which We have signed with
Our Royal Hand. Given at Our Court at Buckingham Palace, the Twenty Sixth
day of May, in the Year of Our Lord One thousand Eight hundred and Forty two,
and in the Fifth Year of Our Reign.

Victoria R.

Rebuffed by the United States, the Republic of Texas sought friends in Europe. King Louis Philippe of France signed this treaty with Texas in 1839 and young Queen Victoria of England recognized the Republic the next year. These and other European powers hoped Texas would remain an independent nation between Mexico and the United States, and their diplomatic and consular agents promoted immigration into Texas and negotiated favorable trade agreements. When the United States finally offered to annex Texas as a state, England and France did all they could to induce Texas to remain independent.

Mirabeau Buonaparte Lamar.

President Houston struggled manfully, often arrogantly, to get the Republic's government functioning; but while he quarreled with Congress and individuals—sometimes from principle, sometimes from pique—and drank more than even unpuritanical Texans approved, his popularity ebbed. His die-hard supporters had no strong candidate to vote for in 1838. Finally Chief Justice Collinsworth, former Attorney General Grayson and Senator Honest Bob Wilson announced their candidacies. This split the Houston faction, which was probably a minority anyhow.

Providence presented the anti-Houstonites a candidate. Vice President Lamar, presiding like a statesman over the Senate—when not poetizing or collecting historical data or talking Texas in Georgia and Alabama—was attracting a great personal following without publicly breaking with the Old Hero. He was personally charming—and he had no important enemies in 1838.

Collinsworth and Grayson died, suicides, before election day, but Honest Bob lived on to win 252 votes. Lamar's landslide with 6,695 votes seemed to him a mandate for a new deal, a reversal of most of Houston's cautious policies.

Surrounded by vigorous young men who shared his vision of a republic "stretching from the Sabine to the Pacific and away to the southwest as far as the obstinacy of the enemy may render it necessary," Lamar confronted Mexico with an option: sign up for peace or "let the sword do its work." Poor Mexico, unable to attempt reconquest or even keep order at home, three times rejected Lamar's offer to pay her well for a quit-claim and she warned the United States that she could annex Texas only over Mexico's prostrate body.

Lamar was as much opposed to annexation as Mexico. Annexation would make his Texas "a tributary vassal to remote and uncongenial communities," would be "the grave of all her hopes"; and prove "that the blood of our martyred heroes had been shed in vain." For three years annexation was a dead issue while Lamar's men tackled other problems and strove "to awaken into vigorous activity the wealth, talent, and enterprise of the country."

Neither Lamar nor his advisers were economists, and the financial condition of the Republic steadily worsened during his three years. There was always hope that the $5,000,000 European loan sought since 1836 would be consummated, hope that the tax yield would miraculously equal expenditures, hope that something would happen to avert national bankruptcy. But the public debt jumped from two to six millions, the amount of unredeemable paper dollars in circulation increased to $3,000,000. In trade these dollars were worth sometimes twelve cents, sometimes two; only the government accepted them at face value. Most Texans did business by barter or with foreign coin and currency.

The new President didn't exactly hate Indians, but he believed that red men could not live peaceably near white settlements. The Indian had to go. In July, 1839, he sent a distinguished embassy to The Bowl, chief of the Cherokees in East Texas—his vice president, secretary of war, adjutant general, two militia generals, and the army commander. They offered to buy the Indians' crops and houses and escort them into Arkansas.

Chief The Bowl, instead of signing the treaty and packing for the journey, rallied his braves. Nine hundred Texans routed them in a series of skirmishes and burned their belongings. They killed The Bowl and sent his hat to "his brother Sam Houston." Surviving Cherokees "fled with great precipitation from the country, thus terminating this vexed question of claim to soil and sovereignty," the war secretary reported from the field. But Chief The Egg and The Bowl's son John fled westward until pursuing Texans killed them Christmas Day. At the cost of some lives and much money, Lamar ended Indian menace in the east and moved the remaining peaceful tribes onto the four-league reservation where their descendants still live as wards of Texas.

In the west the winter of 1839–40 was a bloody one. Spasmodic raids were followed by no-quarter war all along the frontier. In March Lamar's commissioners met twelve Comanche chiefs in the San Antonio courthouse to make peace. The white men gave no presents, as had been customary,

The Battle of Plum Creek.

and announced that the chiefs were to be held prisoners until the Comanches surrendered all their white captives. Within minutes Indians killed seven Texans and wounded eight. Texans slaughtered 35 Indians—chiefs, warriors, women, and children—and took 29 prisoners. The Council House fight was short but, as the official report says, "fruitful in blood." One participant said he was "reluctantly compelled to disembowel his assailant with his bowie knife" although he "had no personal acquaintance with nor personal ill-will towards his antagonist."

The Comanches then mustered 1,000 braves and systematically raided the western frontier from Lavaca Bay to Austin until Rangers and volunteers defeated them at Plum Creek and obliterated their headquarters near present Colorado City. "The rifles, shotguns, and pistols of the white man, in a contest largely hand to hand, with fearful rapidity struck the red man to the earth," reads

Comanches burning the feet of a captive to prevent escape.

the stilted report of the combats that cowed the Comanches and their allies, and taught them that it was better to raid Mexico than the Texas frontier. West Texans knew thereafter how to cope with Comanches.

The line of settlement moved a hundred miles westward as newcomers and old settlers filled in the land Indians had quit. The campaigns cost $2,255,319—a good deal more than Texas had—but Lamar's Indian policy, which Houston declared "utterly falacious," gave Texas years of relative internal peace. It also made workable the policy Texas followed after 1841—limiting Indian trade to established posts and making treaties with the various tribes to keep west of a line from Fort Worth through Menard to San Antonio. Indians remained in Texas but were a decreasing menace for a generation.

Mexican authority in Santa Fe was weak and Lamar was convinced that the New Mexicans wanted to share in the glorious future of Texas. Santa Anna, while prisoner, had agreed that the Rio Grande, mouth to source, should be the Texas boundary and the Texan congress had so decreed it, thus pushing the national boundary through New Mexico and Colorado into Wyoming. At Santa Fe caravans from Mexico and the United States met and traded goods worth millions every year. A Texan customhouse there would pour cash into the empty treasury. It was to be the first step toward pushing the western boundary of Texas to the Pacific Ocean. Congress balked but Lamar recruited 231 volunteers and merchants "to cement the perfect union and identity of Santa Fe and Texas."

Lamar's term was almost over when the Santa Fe Pioneers started in June, 1840, in the general direction of New Mexico.

Six months later the Texans were to learn the outcome.

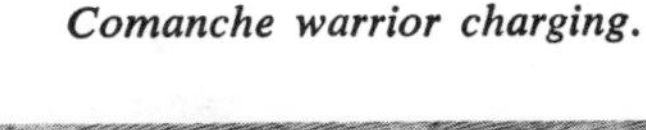

Comanche warrior charging.

Lamar's failures were spectacular and of greater interest to his debt-ridden contemporaries than his considerable achievements. But it was he who laid the foundation for an endowment for public education that is now greater than any other American state has provided. Congress at his urging gave each county four leagues of land for schools and set aside fifty leagues for higher education. "Texas has her captains, let her have her wise men" was his slogan. He also proposed the 1839 Homestead Law—the first such law in the world—exempting a man's home and means of livelihood from execution for debt. And during his presidency recognition of the Republic came from France, Great Britain, Belgium, Holland, and some of the German states. None of them lent her the millions she needed, but they helped in other ways.

William Kennedy, for example, doubled as a colonizer while serving as Queen Victoria's consul in Texas. In 1841 he published a book about Texas that was so good it received the unanimous endorsement of the Texas Congress and enticed many Englishmen to the Republic.

His wily, urbane colleague, Jean Peter Isidore Alphonse Dubois, Count de Saligny, who represented Louis Philippe, received congressional notice, also. In 1840 he asked for a bit of land—3,000,000 acres—west of the frontier line, proposing to colonize 8,000 Frenchmen, operate 20 forts, and monopolize western trade with duty-free French goods. His colonists would pay no taxes but could vote as Texas citizens.

In his embassy at Austin, an island of French culture—wine cellar and furniture, even the chef, imported from Paris—he lobbied the Franco-Texienne bill through the house and almost through the senate "over the fuming bottles and smoking dinners." A French newspaper predicted that "Texas will become, so to speak, an independent French colony . . . costing us nothing." Congressman Sam Houston championed the scheme, but the bill died in the senate under threat of presidential veto.

His hope of fortune and power gone, Saligny vented his anger on innkeeper Richard Bullock, whose pigs had invaded the embassy stable and been killed by the diplomat's servant. On the Texan theory that one who kills a neighbor's pig or steals his horse is a public menace, Bullock

Richard Bullock's Hotel was the best in Austin.

pummeled the man, "bunging up his eyes and phlabotomizing his nose." The Count, regarding pigs as nuisances, declared that Bullock had committed an "odious violation of the law of nations" and called on the sheriff, the courts, the State Department, the President, and the French foreign office for redress. All failed him, and he withdrew to New Orleans, promising to send an ultimatum by warship.

Texans still chuckle over the "Pig War" of 1840 and the fuss-budgety little Frenchman; but it had serious consequences. Saligny's brother-in-law was French minister of finance. He promptly vetoed the $5,000,000 loan Paris bankers had agreed to make Texas.

Relations with France were important. The Texan Legation in Paris, established 1839, had its own seal, and the French chargé in Texas built the finest house in Austin. It is still standing.

During the winter of 1839–40 the ships of the new navy arrived and began making headlines. President Lamar chose Edwin W. Moore as commodore. This twenty-nine-year-old Virginian had enlisted in the United States Navy when he was fifteen—just as the War of 1812 was ending—and he craved more action—and advancement—than that peacetime outfit offered. Lamar gave him his chance and he made the most of it. After patrolling the coast, seizing a few enemy vessels, and mapping the coast, the Texas fleet moved into Mexican waters.

The tropical state of Yucatán, at the south end of Mexico, was asserting her independence. Lamar was sympathetic and the Commodore made Yucatán's cause his own. The $25,000 he obtained there gave his crews their first paydays in months, replenished his stores, and enabled him to send $8,460 to the empty Texas treasury. Here was new hope for wiping out the deficit; a Texan editor prophesied that "the navy could, if permitted to make captures, not only defray its own expenses but support the government."

The September, 1841, election was a referendum on Lamar three months before he left the presidency. Lamar saw the future of Texas more clearly than he did the widespread discontent of his constituents. He saw himself not as a politician intent on petty current affairs, but as a statesman building a republic to last through the centuries. He knew that the panic that spanned his term, not his policies, caused the economic distress.

He also knew that the panic would end someday and that laws he had sponsored would enable Texans to move toward the goal of Big Texas. He was not without vanity, but he prided himself more on his gift of prophecy than his skill at playing politics. Fate granted him little of the luck she showered on Old Sam Houston! When good news came from Santa Fe and the navy returned from Yucatán with casques of gold and James Hamilton brought from Europe the $5,000,000 he was always about to borrow—then Texans could judge him fairly, he thought. But none of these could happen before the election.

For three years Houston had been outdoing everybody in damning Lamar and his friends and all his policies. "He is skillful to destroy his enemy," a senator said of Houston, to prove that "he is the only man that can successfully administer the Govt. of Texas." That is only part of the truth. To Houston, Lamar was only a "Talented Amateur" who won the presidency by default. He lacked the executive temperament, the political know-how and experience that Houston so abundantly had—and his magnificently thick skin.

Houston was an empire builder, too, and he believed that this republic was peculiarly his own creation. Hadn't he signed the Declaration, won the decisive battle, and organized the first government? The trouble was that in the empire he was building there was no place for a man like Lamar who, he felt, couldn't understand that the future can be attained only by solving current problems. It was good politics for Houston to say that Lamar had destroyed all that Houston had built up; but there was conviction in it.

The 1841 campaign struck an all-time low in slander and vituperation. Pitted against the Old Hero was David G. Burnet, whom Houston had regarded as an addle-pated hypocrite since their first meeting, and to whom Houston was a shrewd, unprincipled barbarian. Voters were asked to believe that the General was an opium eater, a

David G. Burnet.

Recruiting for the Texas Navy at Galveston, principal port of the Republic.

drunkard, a coward, a land grabber, father of innumerable half-breed children, and a complete scoundrel. Houston charged Burnet with "foul, unmitigated treason," "political and moral leprosy," hog theft, land grabbing, and sanctimonious hypocrisy. He blamed him for all of Lamar's mistakes—hadn't Burnet been Lamar's vice president and closest adviser?—as well as Burnet's own blunders as ad-interim president in 1836.

There was excitement enough, but the result was never in doubt. Voters subconsciously were pondering two questions: Is the Republic as prosperous as she should be? Is Houston a great man? They answered the first with a resounding No. The second they answered with Yes, three to one.

That September of 1841 Don Martin Peraza arrived from Yucatán to see President Lamar. With Castilian delicacy his revolutionary government agreed "to contribute to the removal of any pecuniary obstacles which might perhaps for the moment embarrass that of Texas in putting her vessels into action" and thereafter to pay $8,000 a month and split spoils fifty-fifty.

The contract was signed, and on December 13 Moore was on his way to the Mexican coast under Lamar's orders "to strike terror among the inhabitants" by capturing towns, levying contributions, and destroying public property. Two days later Houston took over the presidency.

CHAPTER 9

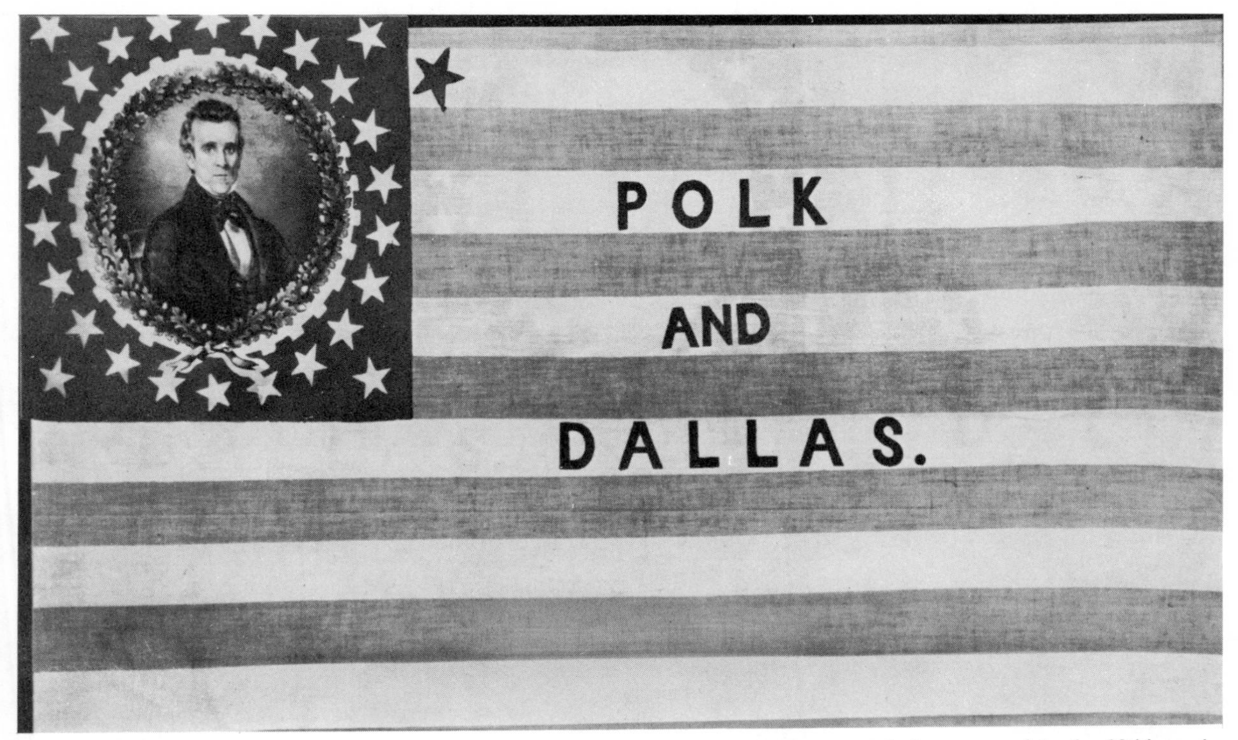

This Democratic banner used in the 1844 presidential election dramatizes the importance of Texas Annexation. The Texas Star, outside, would be added to the other 27 if Polk won.

THE ABSORBING QUESTION

President Houston began his second term by publicly washing his hands of one of the Lamar schemes. In his log office he dictated a peremptory order to Commodore Moore "that the squadron under your command return forthwith to the port of Galveston, and there await further orders." It would be months—four, as it turned out—before the ships could receive it, but it made official His Excellency's disavowal of one Lamar venture while he awaited bad news from another.

He thought the plight of Texas worse than on the day after San Jacinto. In 1836 it was a matter of starting with a clean slate. Now Texas was "without money . . . without credit . . . without character." She was having to grope for national survival through the debris left by the "Talented Amateur." Congress was already using the ax—abolishing two cabinet posts and most of the clerkships, paring salaries, and repealing authority for the $5,000,000 loan. President and Congress agreed on parsimony, little else. Appropriations dropped 90 per cent, from a $2,000,000 average to less than $200,000 a year. The salary account was cut from $173,506 to $32,000. They called it the Retrenchment Congress.

As Congress was finishing its work, news came that all the Santa Fe Pioneers were prisoners of Mexico. Incensed lawmakers promptly reasserted Texan ownership of New Mexico and for good measure added, over Houston's veto, Upper and Lower California and parts of five states inhabited by about two million Mexicans.

Mexico ordered the Texans to abandon their foolish pretense of independence and sent troops into the "Department of Texas" to encourage compliance. In March, 1842, she took San Antonio, seventy miles from the Texan capital, raised the Mexican flag, pilfered for a couple of days, and then retreated. In September an army of 1,400 took the place again. Court was in session when the invaders surrounded the courthouse and captured fifty-three Texans—judge, jury, lawyers, and the men who were there to guard the town. These courthouse prisoners were added to the Santa Fe captives in the far-off Castle of Perote. Of the Texans who flocked to San Antonio too late to fight, 300 crossed the Rio Grande to Mier on Christmas night. Next day they, too, were prisoners. Seventeen of them were executed, the others joined the Santa Fe and courthouse men.

Then the Texas Congress declared war, ordered 10,000,000 acres sold to pay for it, invited private donations, and conferred dictatorial powers on the President. Houston promptly vetoed all this but he did enlist volunteers and order the navy—back from Yucatán long after he ordered it home—to blockade the Mexican coast, without supplying funds for the purpose. And he moved government offices from Austin on the frontier to Houston, near the coast. He ordered the archives moved, too, but when the Austinians, "holding on to the Archivs like death to dead negro," fired on his agents, he managed affairs without his official files. This was the Archive War.

The Texans who invaded Mexico against Houston's orders moved down the Rio Grande in six barges in December, 1842. This "navy" was commanded by T. J. Green, a former general in the Texas Army, who was the historian of the ill-starred Mier expedition.

At Salado, en route to Mexico City, the Texan prisoners overpowered their guards and escaped. A week later they were recaptured.

After their escape from Salado, the Mier prisoners almost starved. At last they found a water hole and killed their fattest horses for food. This, Green said, they did with "a melancholy regret."

The original order to kill all the escapees was modified. Of the 176, the 17 who drew black beans from a barrel were to die.

The 17 Texans who drew the black beans were blindfolded, tied together on a log, and fired upon until all were dead. Next morning the other Mier prisoners started to Mexico City.

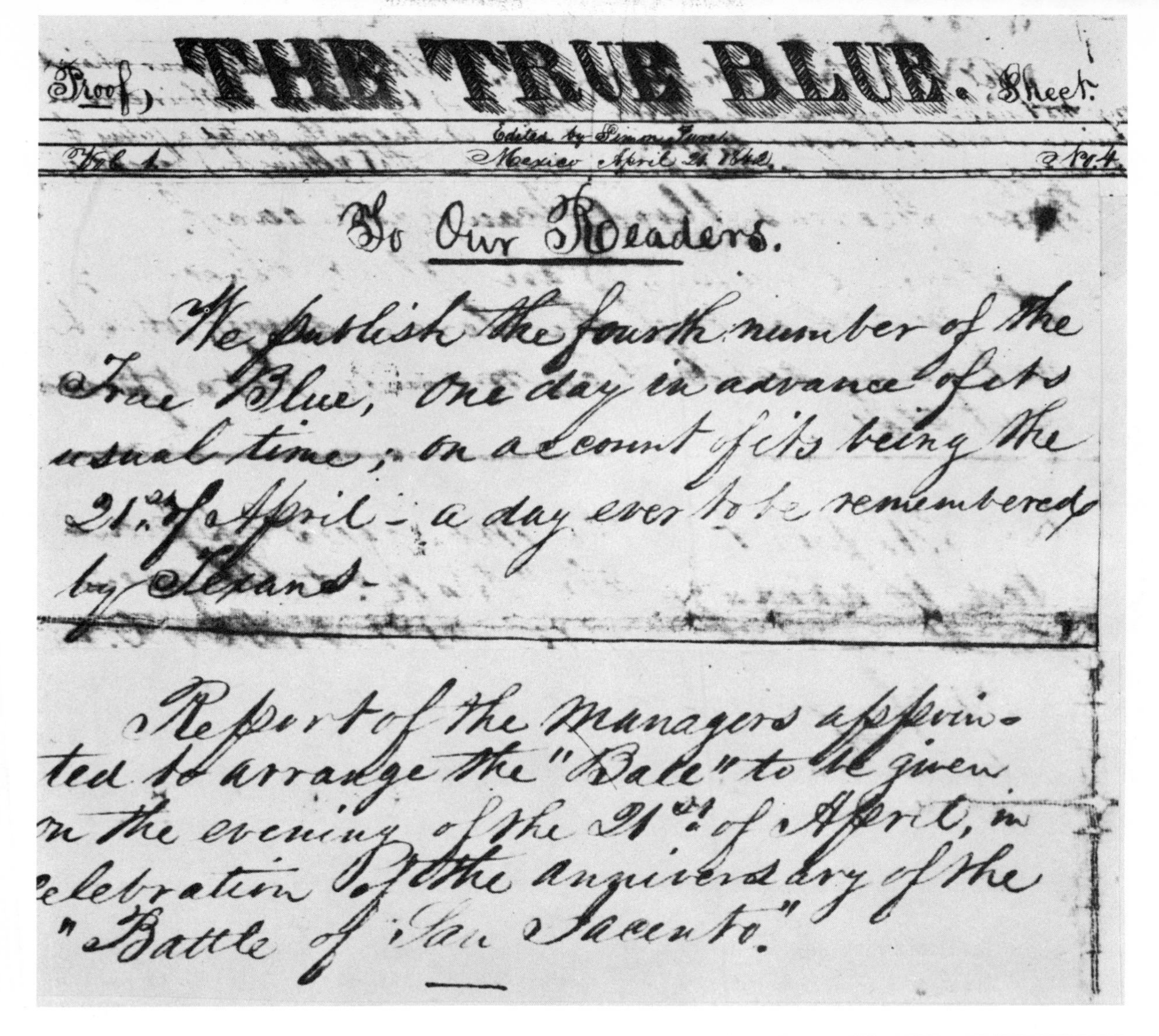

Proof, **THE TRUE BLUE.** Sheet

Vol. 1 Mexico April 2? 1842. No. 4.

To Our Readers.

We publish the fourth number of the True Blue, one day in advance of its usual time, on account of its being the 21st of April — a day ever to be remembered by Texans.

Report of the managers appointed to arrange the "Bale" to be given on the evening of the 21st of April, in celebration of the anniversary of the "Battle of San Jacinto."

Irrepressible Texans, imprisoned in Mexico City, published a manuscript newspaper. This issue announces a San Jacinto ball to be held in the Long Room of the prison "in the immediate vicinity of the residences of the Texan people," and says "A Police will be in attendance to enforce order." Later the Texan prisoners were moved to the Castle of Perote, nearer the coast.

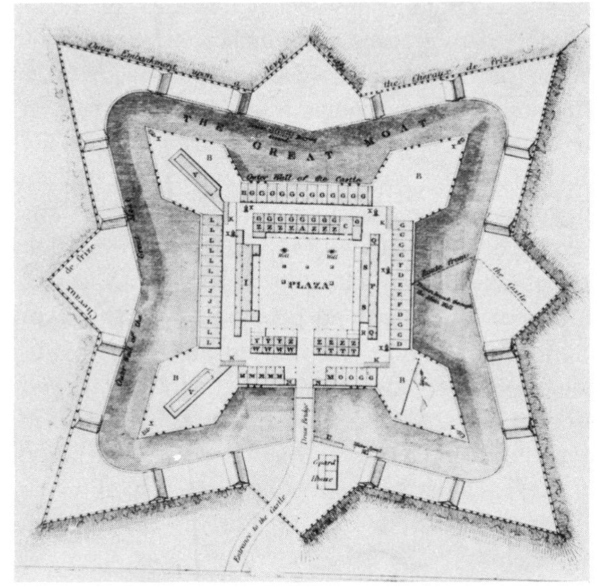

GROUND PLAN
of the
CASTLE OF PEROTE,
DRAWN BY
Charles McLaughlin,
One of the
MIER PRISONERS.

Capitol of the Republic of Texas in the city of Houston.

Commotions in Texas were front-page news in the United States and in Europe and stimulated concern for the Republic's future—if it should have any.

Indian raids, Texan expeditions, and Mexican reprisals, national insolvency, hordes of newcomers starting farms and ranches on cheap land, and a pervading spirit of optimism—these were the contradictory reports from Texas. Statesmen in Washington, London, and European capitals were studying how the vigorous new republic might serve their national interests. Texas was playing an international role out of all proportion to her wealth and 100,000 population. She was strategically located and potentially valuable economically. Most Texans had no notion of the intricacies of foreign affairs, but presidents and secretaries of state understood—and learned to play both ends against the middle. Annexation once more became the Absorbing Question to Texans and to statesmen in Washington, London, and Paris.

The Republic's diplomatic strategist was Anson Jones, a physician who began handling the overlapping crises in 1837, when he was chairman of the House Committee on Foreign Relations. Then he was Texan minister at Washington (where he spent more time with European than American diplomats) and chairman of the Senate Foreign Relations Committee. Now Secretary of State, he knew more about international politics than any other Texan.

His task was to make it possible for Texas either to continue permanently as a sovereign republic, or to get quickly into the Union. Neither would be easy. Jones had no preference, but he knew that Mexican recognition of Texas independence was a prerequisite to either. It was his job to bring that about.

Lamar's failure to negotiate peace convinced Jones that Mexico would recognize Texas only if European powers forced her to do so and then only if she believed that recognition would thwart annexation to the United States.

Jones opened the way for recognition, trade agreements, and other negotiations in Europe when in Washington in 1838 he announced to the world that Texas had withdrawn her offer to join the Union.

In the 1840s visitors in Galveston noticed more European than American ships, and Texas cotton was outselling staple from the Old South abroad. For different reasons, Great Britain and France were developing a strange community of interest with this new republic that lay along the soft side of the United States. Paris and London both wanted Texas to remain independent, not only to block the expansion of Uncle Sam but to open up commercial opportunities. She might become a useful ally, perhaps a satellite.

Politicians in the United States watched this *rapprochement* apprehensively, but neither the Democrats (in power until 1841) nor the Whigs were willing to risk disunity by annexing Texas with its Negro slaves. The kaleidoscope would have to change several times before they could do anything about Texas.

ANNEXATION

OF

THE TEXAS,

A

CASE OF WAR

BETWEEN

ENGLAND AND THE UNITED STATES.

"I know nothing greater or nobler than the undertaking and managing some important accusation, by which some high criminal of State, or some formed body of conspirators against the public, may be arraigned and brought to punishment, through the honest zeal and public affection of a private man."—*Lord Shaftesbury.*

BY

D. URQUHART, ESQ.

LONDON:

JAMES MAYNARD, PANTON STREET, HAYMARKET.

1844.

Would England have to go to war against the United States if Texas were annexed? Daniel Urquhart, a "private man," thought so in 1844.

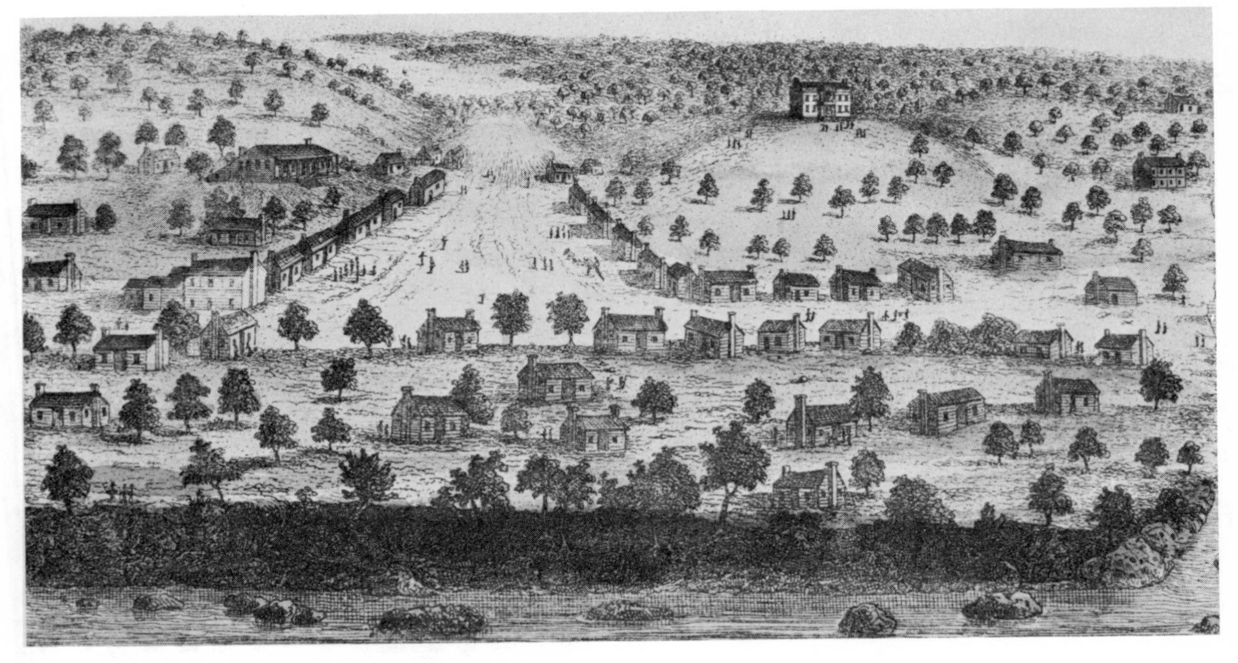

Houston moved the government away from Lamar's Austin and the city languished for several years.

Schooner San Antonio, *Texas Navy, commissioned, 1839, lost at sea, 1842.*

In Texas President Houston meditated often on his navy and its recalcitrance. He was a landsman who never regarded ships as essential to national defense, and he could not forget that Commodore Moore was Lamar's man and, like Lamar, audacious.

The ships had been in New Orleans since May of 1842 and could not move until someone paid the repair bills for which Commodore Moore was surety. It was the President's chance to be rid of the useless navy and in January, 1843, Congress secretly ordered the ships sold for what they would bring.

Moore, ignorant of this, was deep in negotiations with Yucatecans again. In February Señor Peraza arrived in New Orleans with cash for repair bills and a contract for the Commodore on the old terms—$8,000 a month and half the spoils. Moore signed, but before he could sail a Texan agent appeared to suspend Moore and sell his ships. But the Commodore was a persuasive man. In April he sailed for Yucatán and high adventure in Mexican waters, all punctiliously reported to the Texas government. The agent went with him.

When Houston learned of this insubordination, he determined to put an end to Moore's nonsense. On March 23 he proclaimed the Commodore and his sailors pirates and invited anybody, everybody to fetch them home for punishment. "The naval powers of Christendom," His Excellency piously

wrote, "will not permit such a flagrant and unexampled outrage" as Moore was committing. But they did.

None of the ships Moore encountered in the Gulf treated him as a pirate as he busied himself seizing Mexican vessels until June 1. Then the Proclamation of March 23 reached him and he came home under his own power, unchallenged by any "naval power in Christendom." At Galveston he received a hero's welcome, in which His Excellency did not participate. His ships never went to sea again.

After the sheriff refused to arrest him, Moore wrote the navy department that he was "anxious to appear before that tribunal which his excellency, the President, has expressed so much solicitude to the world to have me brought before." The reply was a dishonorable discharge and a list of his crimes—twenty-two of them—ranging from insubordination to piracy and murder. Then nothing happened.

Five months later, when Congress met, Houston was silent as to Moore and the navy but the Commodore demanded an investigation. After hearings Congress found that the President had no authority to discharge Moore without trial, that the "piracy" he complained of had "escaped the knowledge of most, if not all, the elementary writers on international law," that all the charges appeared groundless but a court-martial should hear them. After another eight-month delay a court of militia, generals and colonels with a civilian editor as judge advocate, began the trial. The court sat for three months. The verdict, reached two days before Houston left the presidency, found Moore not guilty on all but four minor charges. His Excellency took time to write: "The President disapproves the proceedings of the Court in toto."

That was the end of the navy. The seamen drifted away, the vessels rotted, the Commodore spent the rest of his life trying to collect what Texas owed him, and Houston gave occasional attention to thwarting his plans. Thirty years later Texas named a county for Moore—a poor little county in the Panhandle, far from the sea.

Anson Jones, the ARCHITECT *of Annexation.*

During Houston's term, annexation prospects brightened. John Tyler, a Virginian and a slaveholder, was determined to add Texas to the Union and in 1843 he was ready to negotiate. At the same time Mexico was seeking a *modus vivendi* with Texas. Santa Anna, in power once more, agreed to an armistice and sent one of the courthouse prisoners home to offer Texas autonomy if she would give nominal allegiance to Mexico.

Secretary Jones proclaimed the facts in phrases so ambiguous that it appeared that Mexico might recognize independence; but there was no ambiguity in his statement that all communications would be handled by British, not American, diplomats.

When the Texan minister at Washington reported Tyler "trying to fix things up . . . stopping to spit on his hands to get a better hold" before offering annexation, Jones replied that "increased prospect of an adjustment of our difficulties with Mexico" would soon simplify negotiation with the

The aged Andrew Jackson was a vigorous advocate of the annexation of Texas. President Tyler also wanted it, and after the United States Senate rejected the annexation treaty in 1844, Tyler induced Congress to annex Texas by resolution in 1845.

I am expecting dispatches from General Howard with great anxiety. Much of the course of the Government will depend upon their complexion. Rely upon it my dear Sir, that nothing shall be left undone on my part to ensure the success of the great measure of annexation. I regard it as the great measure of the age & I seek only to be considered as one of the most desirous for its attainment.

Accept a renewal of my best wishes for a perfect restoration of your health & a prolonged continuance of your life & happiness.

John Tyler.

Genl. Jackson

United States "if," he added significantly, "after this event Texas should continue to desire this annexation." The minister should speak no more of annexation at Washington but dwell on British interest in Texas to "alarm them somewhat."

It worked. By courier came an official invitation to make a treaty of annexation. Houston and Jones wanted to wait for assurance that the United States Senate would ratify the treaty, but impetuous Texas congressmen ordered prompt acceptance of the offer.

The treaty, signed April 12, 1844, would have dissolved the Republic of Texas. The United States would have paid off her debts and carved her land into territories of convenient size and shape that later might become states under various names. That would have been an ignominious ending for a sovereign nation, but the only vigorous objections came from United States senators, who rejected the treaty, 35 to 16, in June—just in time to make it an issue in the election of 1844. James K. Polk declared for "immediate reannexation of Texas" and was elected over Henry Clay who thought such talk "perfectly idle and ridiculous, if not dishonorable."

Political cartoons played a part in the campaign of 1844. This Whig cartoon makes a prediction that did not come true. It shows Henry Clay, opponent of annexation, at the White House, and Tyler, Polk, Dallas, and the Democratic donkey heading for exile in the Republic of Texas. The Democratic cartoon, upper right, *was more accurate. Texas is pictured as a charming, modest lady being welcomed into the Union by Polk and Dallas, while a Quaker tells Clay that he is guilty of the moral delinquencies he imputes to the Texans. Madam Texas hopes that slander will not keep her out of the Union.* Below, *"Texas Shall Be Ours," declare men of Jersey City in a noisy rally.*

Slandered as she is, let him that is without sin, cast the first stone at her!
Welcome, sister, Your Valor has won you liberty and independence, and you have fairly won the right to be identified with the land of the brave, and the home of the free."
Shall the slanders that have been urged against your sister, sever those whose blood flows from the same fountain?
Stand back, Madam Texas! for we are more holy than thou! Do you think we will have anything to do with gamblers, horse-racers, and licentious profligates?
Softly, Softly, Friend Harry. Thou hast mentioned the very reason that we cannot Vote for thee!
DALLAS.
POLK.
TEXAS.
CLAY.
QUAKER.
VIRTUOUS HARRY, OR SET A THIEF TO CATCH A THIEF!

TEXAS SHALL BE OURS

Barrington, President Jones's plantation home near Washington-on-the-Brazos, was the White House of the Republic, 1844–46. It is now in the State Park where the Declaration of Independence was signed and is open to visitors. It is typical of the story-and-a-half plantation houses of the period. Below. *This crude drawing shows the cruder first capitol of Texas at Austin, constructed in 1839. In 1842 President Houston moved the government to Houston, then to Washington-on-the-Brazos, but President Jones returned it to Austin for the inauguration of the state officials in February, 1846.*

Texans also elected a president that fall, but the campaign was not much fun for the voters. Houston, during three years of skirmishes and war threats, delicate diplomacy and feuds with politicians, had his finest hours. He was about to leave the presidency in higher esteem than he had enjoyed since San Jacinto. His secretary of state, Dr. Jones, was pitted against his vice president, General Burleson, and Houston kept silent until the campaign was nearly over.

The only real issue was annexation. Jones, in the midst of negotiations, made no speeches and told no one his stand on the Absorbing Question. Burleson, a weather-beaten frontier hero who "had killed more Indians and Mexicans than any man in Texas," made talks that pleased both Houston men and Houston haters without ever mentioning annexation. At last Houston spoke out, but not on annexation. He only pointed out that Burleson "associated with men opposed to me personally and politically." As for Jones, he added, "I am not opposed to his election."

The choice was between an honest but "very ileterate man" who would be guided by wicked politicians, and a suave physician who killed no Mexicans, practiced medicine while holding office, and was friendly with the British and French envoys. The 13,000 voters chose Anson Jones.

Before his inauguration England and France agreed to force Mexico to recognize Texas if the Republic would remain forever independent. Houston was willing, but the president-elect declined to allow his Republic to become a kind of protectorate.

At Washington, Tyler decided to do part of President-elect Polk's work before Polk took office. With some coaching from Texans, he got Congress to annex Texas by resolution, and on March 1 he rushed the congressional invitation to Texas. If the Republic accepted before the end of the year, she would become a state and keep all her lands and her debts.

In a last-ditch effort to keep Texas out of the Union, the British envoy wrung from Mexico a treaty recognizing Texas as a nation on condition that she never join the United States. At long last,

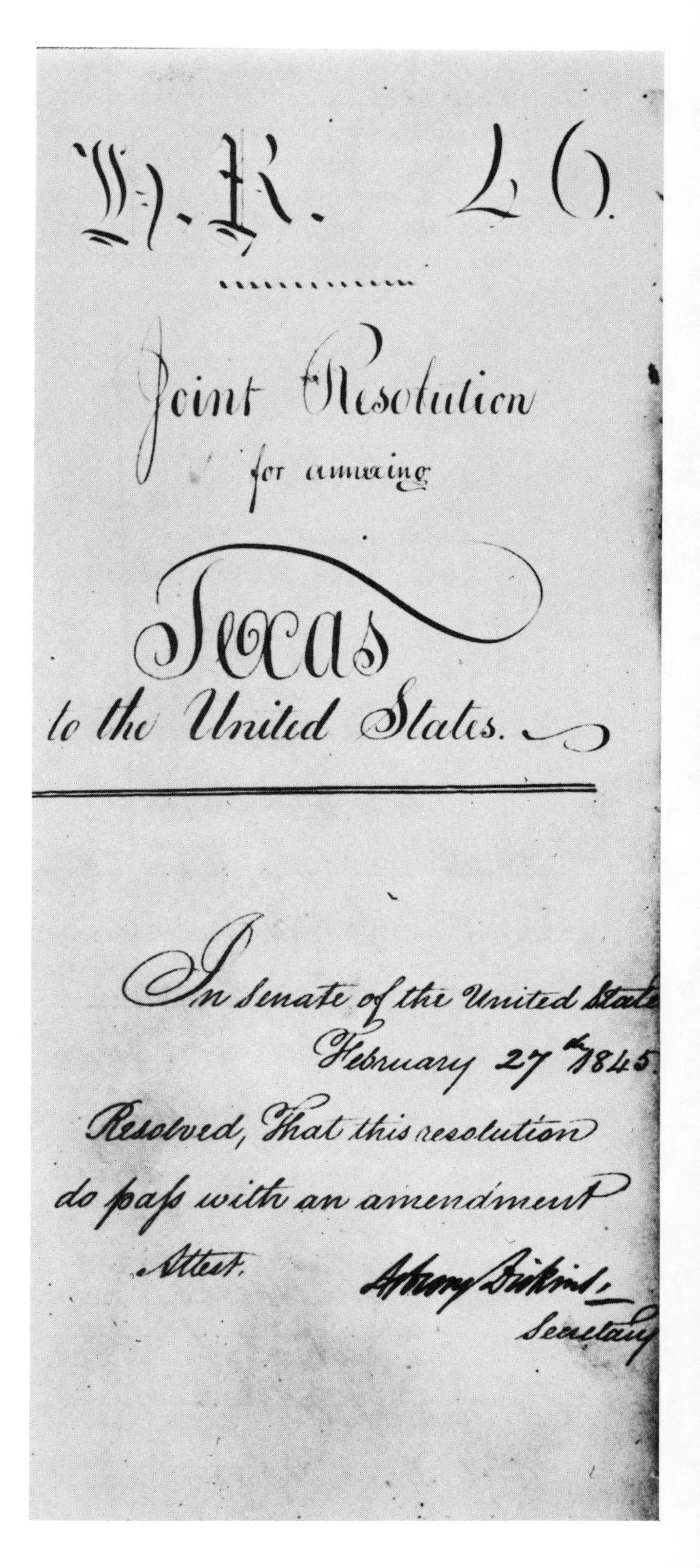

H. R. 46.

Joint Resolution for annexing Texas to the United States.

In Senate of the United States February 27th 1845.

Resolved, That this resolution do pass with an amendment.

Attest. Asbury Dickins, Secretary

in June, 1845, Anson Jones was able to offer the Texans what he had sought for eight years: "the alternatives of peace with the world and Independence; or annexation and its contingencies."

Almost unanimously they chose annexation and its contingencies and damned their president for giving them the alternative. Standing before the log capitol at Austin on February 19, 1846, the last president of Texas solemnly announced: "The great measure of annexation, so earnestly desired by the people of Texas, is happily consummated. . . . The final act in this great drama is now performed. The Republic of Texas is no more." He lowered the flag of the Republic.

Great Seal of the United States affixed to Joint Resolution of Annexation.

CHAPTER 10

A Texan Ranger in the Mexican War.

TENSIONS

Texas officially became the twenty-eighth state in the Union on December 29, 1845. During the next fifteen years her population grew from 125,000 to 600,000; and settlers moved a hundred miles westward into the Indian country. Texas' cotton-corn economy expanded and new towns sprang up in regions newly populated, a few of them connected by railroad. Prosperity was in the air, but friction between the state and federal governments developed early and increased through the years.

First came war with Mexico. Annexation precipitated it, as opponents of annexation had predicted, and the war intensified their anti-Texas feeling. To most Texans it was *their* war, a sort of second war for independence, and 8,000 of them volunteered. Veterans of San Jacinto still remembered the Alamo, and younger Texans gained experience that later would make them able Confederate officers. When General Taylor encamped his army at Corpus Christi and moved toward Brownsville, Mexican forces promptly crossed the Rio Grande. In May, 1846, "American blood was shed on American soil" at Palo

Alto and Resaca de las Palmas, and before Congress could declare war on May 13, Taylor's men were moving toward Monterrey.

Governor J. Pinckney Henderson became a major general commanding Texan troops with former President Lamar at his side. Jack Hays, Ben McCulloch, and Samuel H. Walker recruited Rangers whose audacity vexed General Taylor but won immortal fame as scouts and guerrilla fighters. Texans were in every skirmish of the war, and the Rangers rode with General Scott into Mexico City on September 14, 1847, and reveled in the Halls of Montezuma.

The Texas Congress had annexed the land between the Nueces River (southern limit of Mexican Texas) and the Rio Grande, but never established control over it. When Taylor's army encamped at Corpus Christi, Mexico denounced it as an invasion of Mexico and sent troops to evict the Americanos. Taylor knew, if Mexicans did not, that annexation had made this United States soil; the Mexicans were the invaders. At Palo Alto, twelve miles north of the Rio Grande, 2,200 of Taylor's men routed 4,000 Mexicans, pursued them three miles to Resaca de las Palmas, defeated them again, and drove them south of the Rio Grande. War, President Polk declared, existed by volition of the enemy. Casualties in this first clash were 547 Mexican, 120 American.

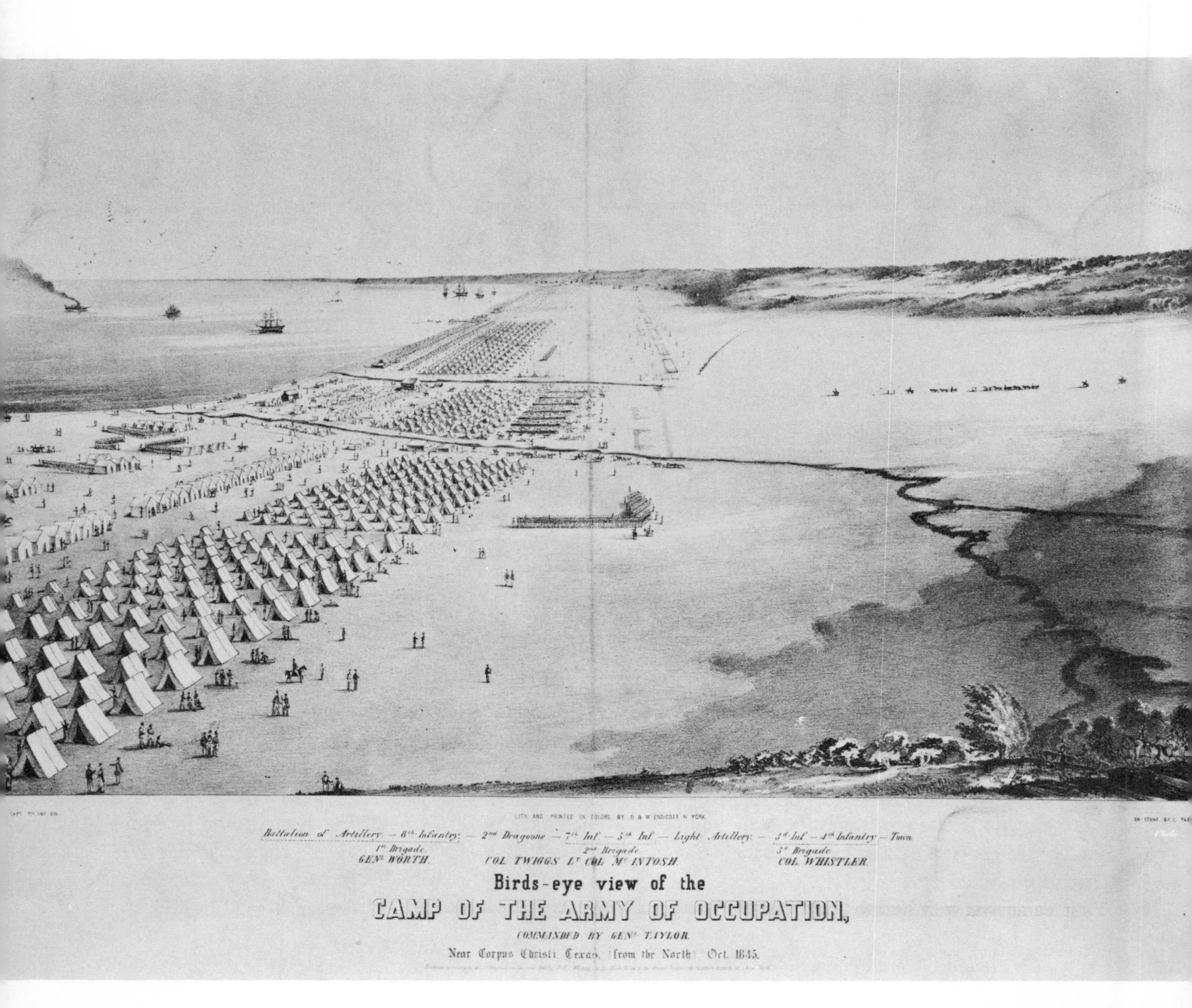

BATTLE OF PALO ALTO.

May 8th 1846, between 2900 Americans, under Genl. Taylor, and 6000 Mexicans, commanded by Genl. Arista. The Mexicans were driven from the ground with great loss. — It is remarkable for being the first battle of the war.

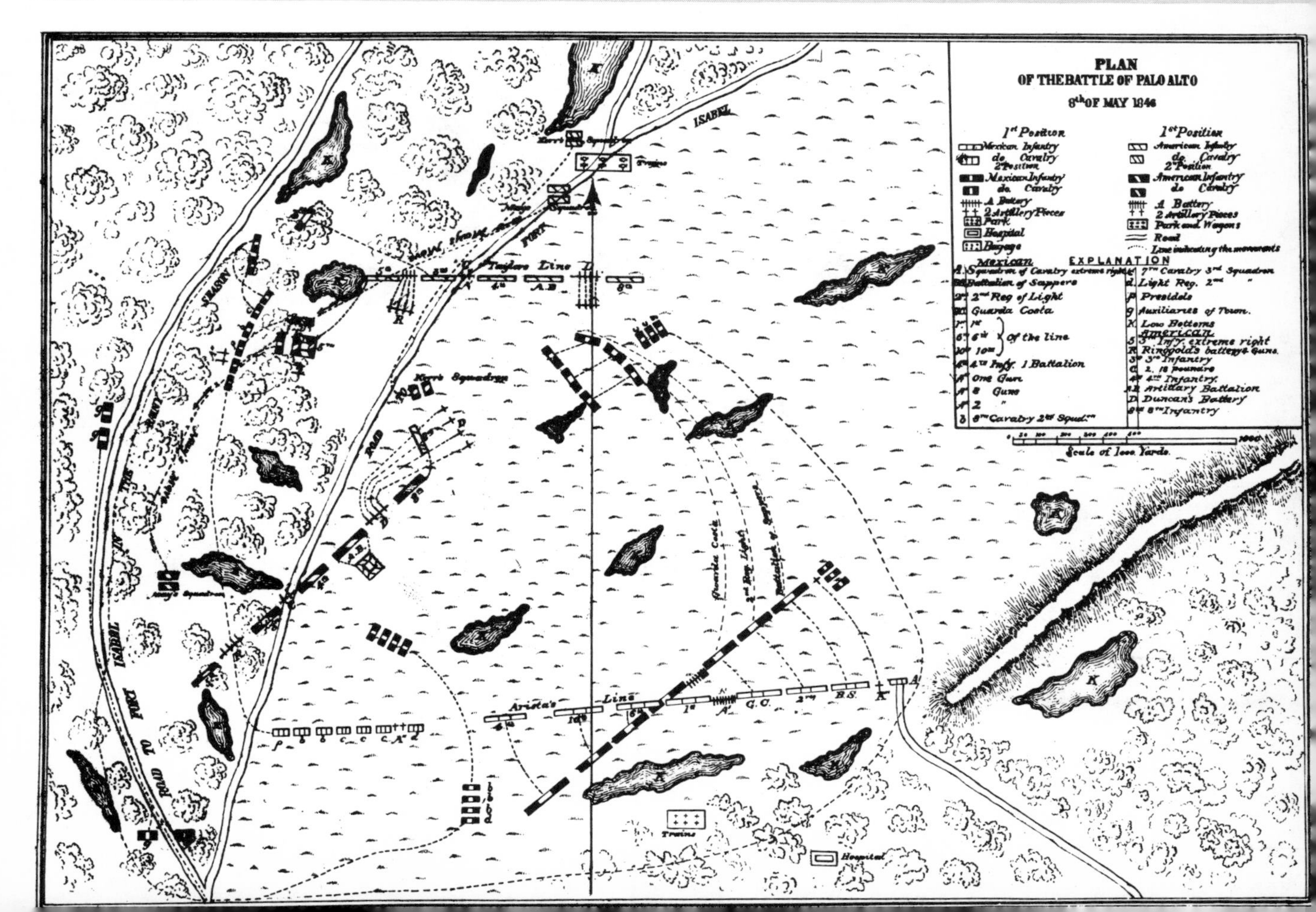

Captain Ben McCulloch, Texas Ranger.

Colonel John Coffee (Jack) Hays, Texas Ranger.

Captain Samuel H. Walker, Texas Ranger.

The Walker six-shooter was a Texan contribution to the taming of the West. Sam Walker, a Marylander, came to Texas and joined the Rangers when he was twenty. Three years later he was in New York showing Samuel Colt how to improve his revolver. The new model—the Walker Colt—became standard equipment for Rangers and its use in the Mexican War made it a favorite with mounted men throughout the West. Walker had "distinguished himself for bravery and coolness" before he was old enough to vote. His was the first Ranger company to join Taylor's army and Walker himself scouted the Mexican positions before the battles of Palo Alto and Resaca de las Palmas. He was killed in battle near the end of the war when he was thirty-seven years old. Long after his death the Texans named a county for him.

Los Diablos Tejanos, as the Mexicans called them, searched Santa Anna's deserted apartments and sent President Polk a magnificent sword cane as a trophy. Once they thought of hanging the Napoleon of the West, but when Santa Anna rode past them in his carriage, he "sat erect, not a muscle of his face moved—if his hour had come he seemed resolved to meet it as a soldier should. . . . The 'ununiformed' representatives of Texas stood motionless and silent. . . . There were no salutations, no ungraceful remarks," a Texan wrote.

In the Treaty of Guadalupe Hidalgo, February, 1848, Mexico handed over to the United States Texas and other lands as far as the Pacific. It fixed the Rio Grande, as far as El Paso, as the southern boundary of Texas, where Texans always claimed it was. But north of El Paso the state and federal governments had overlapping claims—and a federal army had possession.

"OUR ARMY"

ON

THE RIO GRANDE.

INTERIOR OF FORT BROWN.

PHILADELPHIA:

CAREY AND HART.

1846.

Histories of the war with Mexico and sketches of battles were more popular than the war itself in parts of the United States. Buena Vista, where Santa Anna and Taylor fought in 1847, is unique because each commander thought he had lost, then both claimed it as a victory.

Samuel Chamberlain was a joyous soldier. His watercolor sketches, recently discovered, capture the human side of the conflict. Toward the end of the war he spent his time "protecting Mexicans from depredations of American volunteers."

Gen Wool.
Leading the Illinois Reg to the Charge

Rough and Ready
"A little more Grape Cap Bragg!"

The Heroic Charley May.
"Col May your Squadron is thar"

Chamberlain, a six-foot-two teenager with long blond curls, believed the ladies all loved him. Here he depicts a rendezvous with a señorita. He is not in the picture.

While American soldiers "helped Texas win the war," stay-at-home artists and craftsmen in the States did their bit. Whether they approved the war or deplored it, people bought handsome Texian Campaigne dinner services and listened to music that celebrated the victories and war heroes. The china proved more durable than the songs. Even today Texian Campaigne plates are treasured possessions of many families.

Texas entered the Union with all territory "rightfully belonging" to her, which meant everything on the Texas side of the Rio Grande to its source (in Colorado) and northward to the 1836 border of the United States; the Congress of the Republic had so decreed in 1836, and the United States did not question it in 1845.

In 1846 federal troops took charge of this territory without objection from Texas until United States army officers organized a civil government there. In Washington congressmen were talking of barring slavery from all lands ceded by Mexico. Recognition of the Texan claim to land north of El Paso and east of the Rio Grande became imperative.

Texas protested to Washington over the army's actions during the war; when peace came she acted. She created Santa Fe County, Texas, and sent a judge to organize it. He arrived to find New Mexicans petitioning Washington for territorial status and asserting that they had never been part of Texas. Army officers backed them.

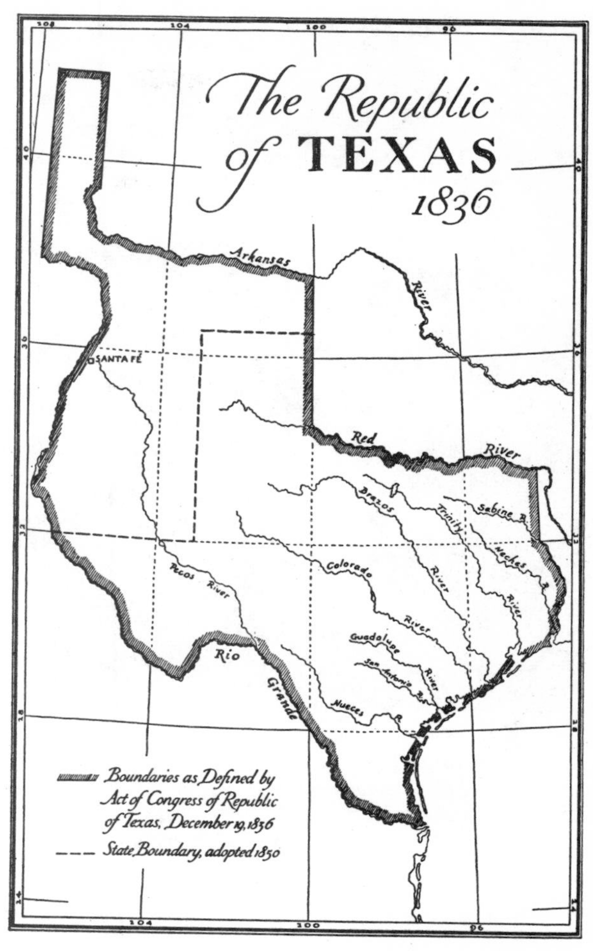

Most of Big Texas was neither settled nor controlled by the Republic or the State, but the Texans lustily asserted claim to all of it from 1836 to 1850.

While politicians were fixing the boundary between Texas and New Mexico, surveyors peaceably mapped the line between Texas and Old Mexico. They camped near Brownsville in 1853.

George T. Wood, a planter-politician since 1839 when a chartered ship brought him and his slaves from Georgia, was elected Governor in 1847. He was a hero of Monterrey.

Peter Hansborough Bell fought in the armies of the Republic, the United States, and the Confederacy. After serving as Governor 1849–53, he served Texas as Congressman.

Governor Wood, a veteran of the recent war, asked the legislature to let him prove Texan claims "with the whole power and resources of the state," promising "there will be no messenger of her defeat." But before he could act, there was a new election and the new governor, P. H. Bell, who had fought in 1836 and 1846–47 for Texan rights, would brook no nonsense from the United States. General Taylor, now President of the United States and no friend of Texas, wanted New Mexico admitted as a state.

That was more than Bell or any other Texan could tolerate. The legislature created additional Texas counties in New Mexico, but again federal officers intervened. Bell was ready to vindicate Texan claims *"at all hazards and to the last extremity."* He asked for troops to quell the "rebellion against Texas" in Santa Fe and to seize the territory.

Newspapers and mass meetings urged secession, but before Texas could resign from this "Union that embraces but to crush and destroy," or send Rangers and militia to New Mexico, the United States offered $10,000,000 for everything beyond Texas' present boundaries—parts of New Mexico, Colorado, Kansas, Wyoming, and Oklahoma. Texas reluctantly agreed, and Bell issued a Thanksgiving proclamation—Texas' first—beginning: "In the language of Holy Writ, 'Now is the Winter of our discontent made glorious Summer.' "

The windfall from Washington settled all the debts of the Republic, paid the state's running expenses six years, built a new capitol, a land office, a governor's mansion still in use, hospitals, courthouses, jails, "internal improvements" that included textile shops in the penitentiary, with enough left over to endow the state's public schools with $2,000,000.

Since 1855 successive Texas governors have occupied this white mansion near the Capitol. It is a good example of the classical-revival architecture known as American Empire. The fluted pillars were adzed from pine logs hauled from Bastrop by slave labor. Governor Pease selected the site and was the first to live there. The spacious grounds are patrolled by Texas Rangers.

Old Fort Brown—The Hospital.
Brownsville.

The settlement assuaged but did not eliminate Texan resentment toward the United States. She was still the biggest state in the Union, and Texan rancor over the Indian problem was deep and articulate.

The crux of this problem was that the Indians were living on public lands owned by Texas but the state had no authority to deal with red men in peace or war. That power passed to the federal government on annexation. The United States owned no land in Texas for forts and reservations and, until the Mexican War ended, had no garrisons for the Texas frontier.

Federal commissioners made formal treaty with some of the tribes in 1846, but a year passed before an Indian agent was appointed—not to protect white settlements but to adjust disputes among the Indians.

When war ended, federal soldiers were placed in widely scattered "forts" along the frontier; most of them were infantrymen—about as useful against mounted Indians as "a sawmill on the ocean," a Texan editor wrote. Texans wanted the Texas Rangers, who had learned the hard way how to make the frontier safe, to drive the red men into Red River. They couldn't understand why the United States preferred the clumsy system she had evolved on other Indian frontiers.

Washington saw nothing special about the Texas frontier; Texans did. It was easy, an editor wrote, to draw a line on a map in Washington and say: " 'Shinny on your side, Mr. Indian.' " But the Indian, unfortunately, " 'no comprende' annexation, 'no comprende' paper treaties, 'no comprende' why his war parties are to hang up their shields and spears and arrows. It is all, from beginning to ending, ridiculously absurd to him." And for other reasons, it was equally absurd to the Texans.

Relying on the benevolence of the Great White Father, the ineptitude of his soldiers in Texas, and the absence of Rangers, the Indians had opportu-

Old Guardhouse—Fort Clark.

Barracks and Hospital—Fort Ringgold.

nities long denied them and they made the most of them. As the tomahawk did its work, neither federal troops nor occasional forays of Rangers could protect the white settlements. It soon became as obvious to Washington and Austin as it was to the frontiersmen that Texas Indians would have to be corralled on reservations, as in other parts of the United States. By a sort of lend-lease Texas provided twelve square miles of reservation land and after 1855 most of the red men eked out a docile, supervised existence on tracts near Graham and along the Brazos until 1859, when they trekked to the Indian Territory (where Oklahoma now is) trailed by United States Army Blue Coats and Texas Rangers.

As the Indian menace subsided, private warfare, lynchings, and reprisals became chronic along the southern border, where Texan authority had never been established. Mexicans seemed a handy target and Texans forthwith charged them with helping runaway slaves and plotting against Americanos; not only that, they were guilty of monopolizing the freighting business between the coast and San Antonio by cutting rates. Some communities evicted all Mexicans and others refused to let Mexican carts pass. There were several lynchings before Rangers quelled the brief, bloody "cart war" in 1857, but even so, peace did not return to the border.

Juan N. Cortina, an enterprising Robin Hood living near Brownsville, turned from cattle rustling to redressing wrongs done Mexicans by Texans. He raided border towns, killed a sheriff or two, raised the Mexican flag, and talked of ridding Texas of all Americanos. Combined forces of Rangers and United States regulars killed 60 of his "army" in December, 1859, and the remainder retreated across the river. When early in 1860 Colonel R. E. Lee advanced to the border with orders to pursue the marauders into Mexico if they re-entered Texas, the Cortina war ended. Thereafter when Cortina rode into Texas, as he continued to do for fifteen years, it was only to steal cattle.

Old Guardhouse — Fort McIntosh.

Despite border troubles, it was a prosperous decade and a half for the new state. The number of slaves grew to 180,000; taxable values rose from 34 to 300 millions; cattle increased ten times over—to 3¾ million head. Texas grew less than forty thousand bales of cotton in 1848; by 1860 it was nearly 500,000. And the role of her cotton planters was way out of proportion to their number; they dominated Texas politics.

Public education, dreamed of since 1839, became a legal reality in 1854 when, under Connecticut-born Governor Pease, $2,000,000 out of the $10,000,000 grant from Washington was dedicated to school endowment. The legislature, pressured by lobbyists who wanted railroads and others who demanded public schools, pleased both

Before the Civil War many East Texans who migrated from the Old South built homes similar to the ones they had left. Most of those that have survived are in towns rather than on plantations. Above, *Wyalucing (which means "home of the friendless") is an excellent specimen of ante-bellum plantation homes. Built in 1850 near Marshall in East Texas, it was the home of Beverly Lafayette Holcombe, a Virginian. There his daughter Lucy was married to Francis W. Pickens, United States minister to Russia and secessionist governor of South Carolina. The sturdy brick mansion was used by the Confederate post office department during the Civil War. In 1880 it was bought by former slaves and presented to Bishop College, whose campus surrounds it.* Right, *Matthew Cartwright, soldier of the Republic, merchant, planter and philanthropist, lived in this beautifully proportioned home at San Augustine until his death in 1870. It is still owned by his descendants. Built in 1839 of Texas pine and cedar, it is still in sound condition. Huge fireplaces upstairs and downstairs warm its high-ceilinged rooms. The column-supported entrance porch is a fine example of classic simplicity. The office in the yard, connected with the house by a latticed porch, is an interesting feature of this and other early homes in East Texas.*

by directing that the school funds be lent to railroad builders and the interest be spent for schools. The state also gave 16 square miles of land for each mile of road constructed. By 1861 Texas had 450 miles of railroad—and was contributing 62 cents per head toward the schooling of her children. That wasn't what Lamar dreamed of, but it was a start.

E. M. Pease recommended the endowment of public schools, directed the building of the new capitol, land office, and governor's mansion. His term as governor was the most prosperous four-year period of early statehood. After he left the governorship, he lived in Woodlawn, a Greek-revival house designed by the architect of the mansion. It is now the home of former Governor Allan Shivers.

Carl, Prince of Solms-Braunfels, was commissioner general of the Adelsverein formed to help Germans migrate to Texas. In 1844 he established Indianola on the Gulf and settled his first colonists at New Braunfels, then returned to Germany. Indianola below *was a busy port for forty years, an army supply depot, and a cattle market. Camels intended for desert transport were landed there in 1856. After two hurricanes (1875 and 1886) Indianola was deserted. The town of Marshall* upper right *began in 1839 on land donated by an illiterate philanthropist named Peter Whetstone. Before 1860 it was called the Athens of East Texas. It had a university, a female seminary, a newspaper, a brick courthouse, and a prosperous citizenry. Marshall subscribed $20,000 to the proposed Southern Pacific railroad which was never built but in 1861 was still advertising: "1,000 Slaves Wanted by Hire or by Purchase" for construction work. Fredericksburg* lower right *began in 1846 when John O. Meusebach led a wagon train of 120 Germans from New Braunfels to the Indian frontier and made a peace treaty with the Comanches which was never violated. Its old buildings are quaint and the* fests *of the old country are still observed there. Its Coffeemill Church, Nimitz Hotel, and Sunday houses (used by farmers when they came to town for church) are distinctive features.*

"We are all Democrats in Texas," wrote Guy M. Bryan, because only the Democrats championed annexation. But rifts soon appeared. Sam Houston, a senator since annexation, voted more often with Yankees than with extreme southerners as the slavery controversy developed. Few Texan politicians approved his course and his personal following dwindled. In 1855 he blessed the Know-Nothing party, which lacked only 4,000 votes of electing a governor in 1855. The Democrats tightened their organization, but split into Unionist and States' Rights factions.

As tension grew throughout the South, Texans recounted their grievances against the federal government and added the threat of abolition. Houston was defeated for the governorship in 1857; but two years later the same Texans who elected a secessionist state legislature placed Unionist Houston in the governor's office. That was the situation at Austin when the crisis arrived.

CHAPTER 11

Official Seal of the Confederate States of America.

THE GLORIOUS CAUSE

Texas declared her independence of the United States on March 2, 1861, twenty-five years to the day after she parted company with Mexico. Geographically she was a part of the New West and also an extension of the Old South. For a decade her grievances had been frontier tribulations, similar to those of other western regions.

Then, within a five-year period, Texas became almost as southern in sentiment as Mississippi or Georgia. She lay within the "natural limits of slavery" and 22,000 of her citizens owned about 180,000 Negroes in 1860. Not many Texans questioned the economic and social rightness of human bondage; most of them expected to own slaves when they were able.

Texan interpretation of national events during the late 1850s convinced most leaders that Texas had nothing to gain and much to lose by remaining in the Union. Sam Houston and a handful of dedicated Unionists tried to stem the rising secession sentiment; but John Brown's raid on Harper's Ferry, the split in the Democratic party, and the election of "the black Republican" Lincoln, in 1860, filled Texans with apprehensions that no amount of logical reasoning could ever hope to dispel. Texans had made up their minds.

JOINT RESOLUTION

RELATIVE TO COERCION.

Be it Resolved by the Legislature of the State of Texas,

That in view of the exigencies of the times, we deem it proper to declare, that when the sovereign States of this Confederacy entered into the compact of the Union, they delegated to the Federal Government no power to compel, by force of arms, obedience by the States to the Federal authority; but on the contrary, such power was expressly denied. That the employment, therefore, of force by the Federal Government to compel any State of this Union to perform its obligations under the Federal compact,or to compel a State against the will of its people to remain a member of theConfederacy, is in violation of the Constitution, a dangerous usurpation of power, destructive of the right of free government and fatal to the existence of the Union itself, which formed of equal and independent sovereignties cannot be as between conquering States and subjugated provinces. That should, (as we have serious reason to apprehend may be in the present condition of the Union,) the Federal Government attempt to coerce any of our sister States of the South, by force of arms, into subjection to Federal rule, we assure such States of the sympathies of our people, and that we shall make common cause with them in resisting by all means and to the last extremity such unconstitutional violence and tyranical usurpation of power.

Passed February 1, A. D. 1861.

M. D. K. TAYLOR,
Speaker of the House of Representatives

EDWARD CLARK,
President of the Senate

On the same day Texan delegates voted Texas out of the Union, the Legislature resolved that under the United States Constitution, no state could be prevented from seceding. They thought their right to own slaves was guaranteed by the United States Constitution, too.

Governor Houston grimly tried to block or delay secession. Legislators, editors, practically all molders of public opinion, were equally determined to get Texas out of the Union. Houston may have been willing to provoke war between the United States and Mexico to avert secession; unquestionably he did all one man could to keep Texas in the Union and, failing that, to keep her out of the Confederacy.

He ignored insistent demands to call a convention. When it met without his sanction, he acquiesced in its actions until it joined Texas to the Confederacy. Then he declined to swear allegiance to the new government and was evicted from office. "It is perhaps meet that my career should close thus," he soliloquized. "I stand the last almost of my race." Two years later his death was reported in two or three Texas newspapers.

Texas entered the Confederacy when the war for southern independence was inevitable. Her first problem was to immobilize the 2,700 federal troops in Texas and seize the $3,000,000 worth of military stores. Luckily, Washington sent no orders to the general commanding, and he yielded to Texan demands. Without the firing of a shot, Federal military power disappeared from Texas.

Twiggs, aged 71, surrendered the federal forces and stores in Texas to state troops in February, 1861. He became a Confederate general.

SURRENDER OF EX-GENERAL TWIGGS, LATE OF THE UNITED STATES ARMY, TO THE TEXAN TROOPS IN THE GRAN PLAZA, SAN ANTONIO, TEXAS, FEBRUARY 16, 1861.

Texas was far from the principal battlefields, but her location made her vulnerable. Indians were still along her western border, and beyond them were Federal garrisons in New Mexico. Civilians and Rangers quieted the Texas Indians and coaxed a few of them into Confederate service. An army commanded by Texans invaded New Mexico and Arizona and held it as Confederate territory for about a year, but after this foray there was little fighting along the western border of Texas.

But on the 2,500-mile coast three of the strangest battles of the war took place. Federal vessels patrolled the Gulf to enforce the blockade, but they could not prevent some ships from slipping in and out of Texas ports. In October, 1862, the U.S.S. *Harriet Lane* and two other ships arrived at Galveston and demanded surrender of the city. Under a flag of truce Confederates evacuated to the mainland and Galveston went by default to the enemy. After the mayor marched between lines of blue-coated uniformed men—city firemen—to hand the naval commander the key to the city, civilians went about their business unmolested. The federal patrol was so inadequate that Confederates visited the city almost nightly without challenge.

That was the situation in the fall of 1862 when General J. Bankhead Magruder took charge of Confederate affairs in Texas. Eviction of the Federals from Galveston was his first project. He reconnoitered the place, then planned an amphibious attack without naval assistance. At the head of Galveston Bay he piled cotton bales around the decks of little river boats and manned them with Texans who could shoot straight. Simultaneously these little "cotton clads" and land forces from the mainland converged on the unsuspecting Federals at daybreak New Year's Day. The cotton clads disabled, captured, or drove off the six Federal vessels, while Magruder's men ashore received the surrender of the city and marched their 600 Federal prisoners to an internment camp. Galveston remained a Confederate port, although Federal control of the Gulf interfered with her shipping.

Confederates made good use of Union equipment captured in Texas.

Four little Confederate "cotton-clads" (double smokestacks) wreck the federal flotilla New Year's Day, 1863, off Galveston.

On the wharf newly arrived Federals are overpowered by Confederates.

General J. Bankhead (Prince John) Magruder directed Confederate operations in Texas, Arizona, and New Mexico and is credited with preventing Federal occupation of the coast. He planned and won the Battle of Galveston, January 1, 1863, by simultaneous land and sea attack. A West Pointer and career Army officer, he joined the Confederates when war began and defeated a small Federal force at Big Bethel in Virginia in May, 1861—the first battle of the war. He arrived in Texas in October, 1862.

Richard W. (Dick) Dowling was born in County Galway, Ireland, in 1838. He joined the Confederate Army as a lieutenant and was in the Battle of Galveston; but his fame was won at Sabine Pass three weeks later. President Jefferson Davis declared: "There is no parallel in ancient or modern warfare to the victory of Dowling and his men at Sabine Pass."

The incredible battle of Sabine Pass came in September, 1863. From Louisiana 5,000 Federal troops and four gunboats embarked for Texas to begin a campaign "of the most brilliant and lasting character." They would enter the Sabine River and sweep through the state. General Magruder dispatched Lieutenant Dick Dowling, a young Irishman who kept a Houston saloon, to spike the six Confederate guns that guarded the Pass. Instead, Dowling with less than 50 men manned the guns and when the flotilla came into range, opened fire. One by one the men aboard the Federal gunboats took to the water; one by one the ships raised white flags.

At the end of forty-five minutes Dowling "raised a white handkerchief on his sword" and advanced to receive the surrender. The Union commander had neglected to bring his sword and Dowling escorted him back to get it. This surrender had to be carried out in proper form. The Federals lost 19 killed, 9 wounded, 37 missing, 315 prisoners; the rest fled back to Louisiana. "Our loss," the Confederate report reads, "was, strictly and positively, nobody hurt. Not a single man received even a scratch." Thus, a Texan wrote, did "a boy-like chief with forty men and six old guns . . . stem attack by men of war." There was no further contest there.

Panorama of the Seat of War.

BIRDS EYE VIEW

OF TEXAS AND PART OF MEXICO

Battle of Sabine Pass

THE CONFEDERATES EVACUATING BROWNSVILLE, TEXAS.—[SKETCHED BY AN ENGLISH ARTIST.]

At the south end of the coast in November, 1863, 6,000 Federals took Brownsville and held it until spring, then withdrew.

After the war had officially ended at Appomattox, 300 Union troops returned to Brownsville. At Palmito Ranch nearby Colonel Rip Ford attacked them on May 13 with artillery and rebel yells, killed 30 and captured 113—and learned from his astonished prisoners that the war had ended five weeks before. The Confederates, having lost the war, won the last battle.

More Texans than voted in 1861 had flocked into the Confederate armies—about 60,000 of them—and served in every campaign. About 2,000 Texans joined the Union army and a few attained high rank; but it is the boys in gray that modern Texans remember. Albert Sidney Johnston, a Texan since 1837, was a full general; another Texan, John B. Hood, a lieutenant general; three were major generals; 32 were brigadiers, and 97 were colonels.

Except for loss of man power, Texas suffered little by the war. Crops were good each year, and Union forces were never able fully to blockade Texas ports or cut off trade with Mexico. Thousands of bales of Texas cotton got to Europe, and a small stream of money flowed back into Texas. When the war ended, Texas had more hard money and foodstuffs than all the rest of the Confederacy—which wasn't much—and a number of war-created small industries—salt, iron, textiles, and small manufactories—which, had the South won, might have developed rapidly. But the atmosphere of defeat did not stimulate initiative and enterprise.

As ex-Confederates drifted back home—no severance pay, no GI bill of rights, no transportation allowance—they were dispirited but not hopeless. They knew how to start from scratch and they could do it again if they must. Not many of them anticipated the complexities that lay ahead, for them and for Texas.

A TEXAN RANGER.

We publish above a sketch, by one of our most reliable artists, of a TEXAN RANGER. A gentleman, just from Richmond, gave the following account of these redoubtable warriors:

Ben M'Cullough's Texan Rangers are described as a desperate set of fellows. They number one thousand half savages, each of whom is mounted upon a mustang horse. Each is armed with a pair of Colt's navy revolvers, a rifle, a tomahawk, a Texan bowie-knife, and a lasso. They are described as being very dexterous in the use of the latter. These men are to be pitted against Wilson's Zouaves and M'Mullin's Rangers.

In wartime even a "most reliable artist" and a gentleman "just from Richmond" could be expected to exaggerate some of the features of the Texas Rangers and their equipment. But the 1861 photographs of these young Texans ready to "repel the invaders" show not only their grim determination but the variety of portable arms they carried with them into the Confederate Army. Members of a pioneer East Texas family originally from Virginia, these brothers were John H. Roberts and Benjamin Roberts of Nacogdoches, who served throughout the war.

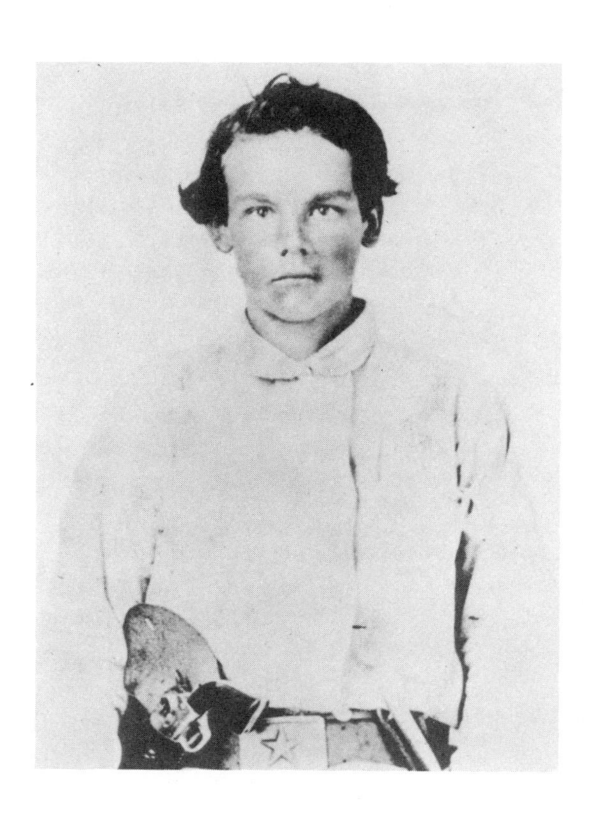

John S. (Rip) Ford was the Confederate colonel who won the last battle of the war at Palmito Ranch, in May, 1865. A Texan and a soldier off and on since 1836, he was also a physician, congressman, editor, cattle inspector, mayor of Brownsville, state senator, and superintendent of the Texas Deaf and Dumb School.

CHAPTER 12

THE WAY BACK

The ordeal of Reconstruction lasted nearly ten years, and Texans found it harder to endure than the war itself. It began June 19, 1865, when a Union general declared the slaves free and took charge of Texan affairs. Next month A. J. Hamilton, a Texas Unionist, became provisional governor by appointment of President Johnson. He invited Texans to take an oath of allegiance to the United States, then to select delegates to rewrite the Constitution.

This was promptly done, and on June 4, 1866, the Texans elected J. W. Throckmorton their governor. He had voted against secession, then became a Confederate brigadier. He defeated Unionist E. M. Pease, who had been governor 1853–57. On August 20 President Johnson declared insurrection in Texas ended, and most Texans thought Reconstruction was over. But when they elected ex-Confederates to Congress, the house and senate refused to seat them and, on March 2, 1867, placed major generals in charge of southern states until new state governments of the type prescribed by Congress could be formed. Texas had to begin all over again.

Governor James W. Throckmorton.

Ex Dpt Texas
Austin August 7th 1867

E. M Pease Esqr
Dr Sir:
I have the honor to acknowledge the receipt of your communication, with enclosure of extract from Special orders No 105 issued from the Hd Qrs ~~Dept~~ the Fifth Military district of date July 30th 1867, and in answer have to say that ~~I will be ready~~ it will suit my convenience to turn over to you at 10 o'clock A.M. tomorrow the Executive office of this State and the archives thereof.
Very Respectfully
Yr. Obt. Servt
J W Throckmorton
Governor of Texas

Austin Texas
7th August 1867

J W Throckmorton Esq
Dear Sir
I have the honor to enclose you a copy of my appointment as Governor of Texas and also to inform you that I have this day taken and subscribed the oaths of office prescribed by the Constitution of this State and the laws of the United States.
Will you please inform me if it will suit your convenience to deliver the office and its records at 10 o'clock AM on tomorrow
Very Respectfully
Your Obt Servt
E M Pease

When James W. Throckmorton took the Governor's oath on August 9, 1866, he thought he was to serve two years, but he was mistaken. General Philip Sheridan found him "an impediment to Reconstruction" and appointed E. M. Pease Governor. Pease was sworn in August 7, 1867, and immediately asked Throckmorton when he could take possession of the office. Throckmorton, still signing himself Governor of Texas, first wrote "I will be ready," then changed it to "it will suit my convenience" to surrender the office and its records "at 10 o'clock tomorrow." Then, to avoid any possible misunderstanding, he inserted "A.M." after the 10. Thus began the second bitter phase of Reconstruction.

By August General Sheridan, commanding Texas and Louisiana, had removed Governor Throckmorton and the justices of the Supreme Court and appointed Pease, whom Texans had rejected four to one, governor. Then the new Negro citizens and such white men as would swear they had given no aid or sympathy to the Confederacy elected another convention. Nine Negroes and only a dozen "carpetbaggers" helped draft the new constitution. It was a radical document of which few old Texans approved, but it satisfied Congress. On March 30, 1870, Texas ceased to be a military district and became a state again.

"The railroad depots everywhere were crowded with Negroes, immigrants, tourists, and speculators" during Reconstruction.

Railroad construction boomed, giving Texas continuous rail routes from the Gulf north to the Midwestern cities and eastward to the Trans-Mississippi rail lines. At left, *a crowded "through car" from Missouri to Texas.* At right, *a train passing through Indian territory (Oklahoma). The covered wagons and the long trail of cattle headed North show that the iron horse had not yet monopolized transportation. Texas was generous to railroad builders.*

"Good Bye."
WE'RE GOING TO KANSAS AND TEXAS.

From the Texan point of view, it was the wrong kind of state—governed under a constitution which centralized executive and judicial power in the hands of Governor E. J. Davis, who had been a Union general, and who intimidated the legislature and declared martial law on whim. He was a southerner and had lived in Texas thirty years, but few citizens approved of him or his theories and practices. To them, he was a despot and his administration incredibly corrupt. Even former Governor A. J. Hamilton, a fellow Republican, declared that Texas was "governed by E. J. Davis as completely as if there were no constitutions, state or federal."

In 1873 the nightmare of radical rule came to an end. In January a Democratic legislature began repealing Davis' legislation and curbing the Governor's powers. In November former Confederate Richard Coke defeated Davis for the governorship, two to one, and next January he "returned the government to the people."

A new constitution was adopted in 1876, and it is still in force. It is a long, detailed document that reduces the governor's role to little more than a figurehead, makes practically all officers elective and insures public parsimony by limiting the state debt and tax rate. Under it no Republican has been elected to state office. The Democrats have controlled Texas under a constitution that despite frequent amendments is full of early nineteenth-century notions. After 1876, few great names enliven the political saga of the state, and few great issues have shaken the electorate. For almost a century Texans have only sporadically been interested in politics. Their attention and energy have been directed elsewhere.

Old Texans forgave many of the officers sent from Washington to supervise Reconstruction, but not General Sheridan. They knew that he was only doing his assigned military duty when he ushered in radical rule and did not hold him personally responsible. They hated him for what he said: "If I owned Texas and all Hell, I would rent out Texas and live in Hell." Years later he apologized.

CHAPTER 13

TEXAS BRAND

Until 1870 the western half of the state was inhabited by Indians, buffalo, and cattle, with only one white man per ten square miles to bother them. It became the Cattle Kingdom, which bred steers and fortunes—and legends and folklore that have outlasted the Kingdom itself. By 1900 the farmers were pushing into the range country and half a century later they had practically taken it over. The region that had 40,000 inhabitants in 1870 had 2,000,000 in 1950 and most of the cattle were elsewhere. Few other regions in the world ever underwent such a complete transformation as West Texas during a single life span.

Indians, pushed steadily westward by white men, made their determined if not heroic last stand there against United States cavalry and the Texas Rangers. The Ranger captains were as mild as Methodist preachers except when dealing with red men. The Army re-established Texas forts, abandoned since 1861, and sent such generals as Sherman, Marcy, and Ranald Mackenzie to maintain peace. For a decade, until 1875, the Indians resisted bloodily; then they trailed into reservations in Indian Territory to harass Texans no more.

The days of raiding and scalping were over.

Buffalo Hunters' Camp.

The buffalo, which had kept the plains Indians alive for centuries, were exterminated by 1880. It was not the Army, the Rangers, or the farmer who rid Texas of the humpbacked cows, but the professional hunter who sold the hides to tanners as far away as England, and occasionally marketed the meat, which the Dallas *Herald* declared "is the sweetest kind of meat and is tender"—and sold for three cents a pound. On a single day in 1877 one store sold buffalo hunters $2,500 worth of guns and ammunition; during two months that winter 100,000 hides were shipped from Texas; two years later the buffalo, like the Indian, was gone. A few stray animals grazed about among the cattle that white men were driving onto the plains; but the market for the buffalo was the city zoo, not the tannery or the packing house.

Texan buffalo hunters. An observer found their camps "picturesque but not oversavory."

The land the Indian and the buffalo vacated became the fabulous Cattle Kingdom. Cattle and horses, brought from Spain by the conquistadores, had been in Texas since 1690, multiplying and spreading over the grassy regions; but cattle tending was not a major occupation until after Anglo-American colonization. For forty years after 1820, many a man who came to Texas to plow and plant became a cowman simply by branding wild cattle and grazing them on vacant land. Texas was definitely "cow country," and it remains "cow country" to this day, with more beef cattle than ever before. But the period during which the cowboy became a folk hero—as distinctive a western type as the trapper or the Indian trader—lasted little more than a decade. He was the last and most durable western stereotype; his popularity increases year by year. There were always hundreds of plowmen for every cowboy, but to Americans and foreigners alike the cowboy symbolizes Texas.

Descendants of mission cattle, unattended, propagated prodigiously in the scrubby land of scant water between San Antonio and the Rio Grande. There the industry began on little isolated ranches stocked with cattle got by merely lassoing and branding them. They were long-legged, longhorned, and tough—"fifty times more dangerous to footmen than the fiercest buffalo," an army officer found. Every unbranded yearling was fair game; they were called mavericks after a distinguished signer of the Texas Declaration of Independence, some of whose cattle strayed off without his brand on their flanks.

Texas Longhorns descended from the Spaniards' cows.

The Longhorn was hard to tame and tough to eat.

From the brush country the cattle industry spread across Texas and into other states, and the rangy longhorn mingled with the gentler, fatter stock that settlers brought from the United States. Later breeds brought better prices and pure longhorns died out—but not before they, too, had become a Texas symbol. It was the longhorn that produced the cowboy.

Before 1860 as many as 60,000 Texas cattle were annually driven west to California, or east to Louisiana and Mississippi, or even as far north as Ohio; but the war closed these outlets. By 1865 Texas had eight cows for each human inhabitant. Hundreds of new names—Goodnight and Waggoner among them—were added to the pioneer Kinneys, Kenedys, and Kings on the roll of cattle kings. Ranching spread north and west of Dallas, Denton, and Forth Worth.

By 1876 the High Plains adjacent to New Mexico was the principal cattle kingdom, with minor principalities in other parts of the state and in New Mexico and Colorado.

Before 1890 Texas had moved 10,000,000 cattle and 1,000,000 horses to northern markets, along trails famous in legend and song. Exploits of the thousands of cowboys who rode these trails made newspaper copy and captured public imagination. Cowboys who were trail drivers were more vivid and colorful than those who did the humdrum work of the range, and were better publicized.

On the range the cowboy was a resolute and lonely man, contending hourly against the unfriendly forces of nature and stubborn beasts. His partner was his horse, whom he taught and from whom he learned the psychology of the cow. Man and horse were a working unit, neither worth much without the other, each generously fitted out with his own special professional equipment.

For the man, a hat—a broad-brimmed Stetson after the 1870s—that protected him from rain and sun, and could double as a feed bag, canteen, washbasin, even as a weapon against unruly cattle. Around his neck a loosely knotted bandanna —less a gaudy ornament than a handy tool: it was his dust filter, towel, napkin, kerchief; sometimes a blindfold for a calf or a bandage for a wound.

Over his cotton flannel shirt, as loud as his bandanna, he sometimes wore a leather vest but seldom a jacket. Trousers were tight-fitting blue denim, put together with yellow thread and copper rivets, the legs stuffed inside his boot tops. His wide belt supported his pants and his Colt .45 and carried cartridges and money if he had any.

Breaking a horse for cattle herding was a tedious job that demanded strength, agility, and a great deal of "horse sense."

His boots were a special mark of distinction, designed for utility as well as beauty. Their pointed toes, soft soles, cross-stitched fancy tops, and high heels not only set him aside from the man on foot, but enabled him to do his work better. In brush country he wore chaps ("hair pants" or "riding apron"), leather shields from belt to ankle, often fringed and ornamented. Spurs and sometimes gauntlet gloves completed his working costume. On the range or on the trail he sang: "I carry my wardrobe all on my back." He seldom bathed and rarely shaved; he had no reason to change clothes.

For his horse, work gear was bridle and saddle—and the things the saddle supported. The bridle was plain, without pendants that might interfere with roping; but the saddle was usually as handsome as its owner could afford—tooled leather, silver pommel and decoration, fancy stirrups—but it was his workbench, not a showpiece. Many a cowboy had a "ten-dollar horse and a fifty-dollar saddle" because the saddle was his dearest possession, his indispensable tool. The lariat, coiled, was tied to the right side, his scabbard and short rifle on the left. When he had to get his own grub—rations, coffeepot, and skillet, rolled in his blanket, were tied securely behind the cantle.

After the war, as the size of herds increased to an average of three thousand the chuck wagon came into general use. Drawn by four or six horses, driven by the camp cook (who could also barber, pull teeth, and doctor), it hauled bedrolls and sustenance for the crew with an economy of space that a house-trailer manufacturer could envy. Canned and dried foods and things killed along the way enabled the cook to concoct delicacies like son-of-a-gun stew and sourdough biscuits. Milk was lacking from the diet; milk was for the calves.

All activities revolved around the chuck wagon with its canvas spread wide to make a broad shelter. At sunup the men ate there, some returned at noon for food, and all showed up at dusk for supper. Eating was an animal necessity, grimly and silently attended to. But when they had finished supper, they threw their tin plates and cups into the "wreck pan" and relaxed. That was the time for wrassling, practical jokes, tall tales, and songs—or just gazing at the stars and wondering—until time to take out the bedrolls. And such tales and such songs! Not all have been recorded, but those that J. Frank Dobie and John A. Lomax

Cattle Moving Up the Trail.

compiled prove that the cowboy forged his own language and coined his own imagery. Work was done; tomorrow would be another day and another dollar—an exaggeration in the 1880s when $15 or $20 a month was standard wage.

Drives began when the grass turned green and continued until cold weather came to Dodge City and the other trail-ends. To the variety of owner brands, a road brand was usually added for identification en route. Distance between watering places fixed the rate of travel and the cattle, moving in a long and sinuous line, grazed and fattened as they ambled twelve or fifteen miles a day toward their death place. A horse worked half a day, then rested two or three days; but every man had a horse saddled and ready at all times. Few operations in that premechanized day were as efficient as trail driving, and no modern discipline is as firm as that of the trail boss. The methods and terminology of the Texas Cattle Kingdom became standard in the West as Texas breeding stock and cowmen moved into new kingdoms in Montana, Wyoming, the Dakotas, Indian Territory, Kansas, and Nebraska.

The heraldry of the range remains a part of the Texas tradition, and some Texans who never owned a cow or rode a horse display their grandfather's cattle brand on their mailboxes and station wagons. Brands of the Spanish period were pictographs, with weird curlicues added by successive generations. As the industry grew, owners devised more than five thousand distinctive, nonalterable brands and recorded them at the courthouses; and hide inspectors were added to the long list of elected officials. Blacksmiths hammered out initials, numerals, fishtails, buzzards, coons on rails, anvils, trunk handles, spurs, rocking chairs, frying pans, and hundreds of other designs that at roundup time were burned into calves' hides.

Ability to "read brands" is a proud accomplishment of Texas youngsters, who know that a leaning letter is "tumbling," a horizontal letter is "lazy."

"They threw their ropes as a man tosses a quoit, drawing it back at the instant it closed over the horse's head. . . . The pony was trained to suit its gait to that of the animal it was pursuing, and to turn and dodge with it, and to stop with both forefeet planted firmly. . . ."

Even while the Cattle Kingdom was forming, nesters were encroaching on its eastern borders to lay foundations for a new agricultural empire. From other parts of Texas but principally from the Old South they trekked westward after 1865, lured by free land—160 acres for a family, 80 for a single man. By wagon, horseback, and ultimately on excursion trains they came to replace cow culture with plow culture, each year expanding the farm frontier at the expense of open range.

Railroads did not crisscross the plains until the decade of the 1880s, but the new Texas fever began earlier when railroads and steamers announced half fare to Texas to immigrants from the States and hauled their baggage free. Colonization societies in Pennsylvania, Indiana, Ohio, and other states bought tracts of 50,000 to 100,000 acres for German, Quaker, and plain American farmers. In 1874, 50,000 Alabamans reportedly "fled into northern and western Texas." So rapid was settlement that the Legislature in 1876 created 54 western counties in a single act. As rail lines pushed through the plains, they brought farmers from everywhere to buy their bounty land and merchants to build the new towns they created. Open range was doomed. The windmill and barbed wire were solving the major western problems of fencing and water.

Barbed wire was not a Texan invention, but Texans were its principal buyers. In 1879 Bet-A-Million Gates built a barbed-wire corral in front of the Alamo during a cattlemen's convention and dared anyone to find a steer that could break through it. Many tried but none succeeded. His factory couldn't make wire fast enough to fill all the orders. Ranchmen fenced first to protect waterholes from trespassers and to keep rustlers away from their herds. Then farmers fenced to keep range cattle off their crops. All over the plains roads and trails were blocked by barbed wire.

This led to the brief but costly fence-cutting war of the early 1880s. Forthright Texans began cutting their way through obstructing barbed wire; less forthright ones organized such gangs as the Owls, Blue Devils, and Javalinas to cut fences, rustle cattle, and burn pastures by night. After some $20,000,000 worth of damage had been done, a special session of the Legislature decreed prison terms for fence cutters and the Texas Rangers moved in to end the war, but not before the commotions had almost stopped immigration.

By 1890 the Cattle Kingdom was a memory. Some great ranches, fenced with barbed wire and owned by "foreign" capital, remained, but the open-range cowman was gone, squeezed out by the big ranches and the encroachment of fenced farms. The state looked on with official approval. Said a commissioner of the General Land Office: "One good home for a child is worth more to the country than many ranches with a thousand cows . . . ; the cry of one child is more civilizing than the 'bleat' of ten thousand calves. . . ."

The struggle between cowman and farmer was won by the man with the plow and West Texas was "no longer the land of the longhorns and h-ll." And operators of big ranches—there are still about twenty in Texas—have found a community of interest with the farmers whose wheat and cotton fields fringe their fenced pastures.

Finding breaks in the fences and mending them before the cattle found them was a necessary but unglamorous chore after the 1870's, and it was a two-man job that was hard on the dispositions.

BEADLE'S HALF DIME Library

Vol. XIX. $2.50 a Year. PUBLISHED WEEKLY BY BEADLE AND ADAMS, No. 98 WILLIAM STREET, NEW YORK. Price, 5 Cents. No. 484.

COMANCHE DICK AND HIS THREE INVINCIBLES

OR,

YANKEE EPH'S PRAIRIE CRUISE.

A Romance of Old Texan Days.

BY HENRY J. THOMAS.

CHAPTER I.

THE PRAIRIE FIGHT.

LOOKING northwest on that summer evening, the three rangers saw a lurid light against the sky, as if made by some burning building, or the beginning of a vast prairie conflagration.

The hunters reined up their horses side by side, and for a few minutes neither of them spoke, while their eyes were turned toward the illumination, in their earnest seeking to understand its meaning.

"That's one thing sart'in," exclaimed Black

ALMOST SIMULTANEOUS WITH A PECULIAR WHISTLE OF BLACK GEORGE, THE THREE MUSTANGS DROPPED FLAT UPON THE GROUND, THEIR MASTERS IMITATING THEIR EXAMPLE.

A TEXAS COW BOY

OR,

FIFTEEN YEARS

ON THE

Hurricane Deck of a Spanish Pony.

TAKEN FROM REAL LIFE

BY

CHAS. A. SIRINGO,

AN OLD STOVE UP "COW PUNCHER," WHO HAS SPENT NEARLY TWENTY YEARS ON THE GREAT WESTERN CATTLE RANGES.

SIRINGO & DOBSON, Publishers,
CHICAGO, ILL.
1886.

THE LEGEND AND THE REALITY

"Thrillers" about Texas and its cowboys were best sellers for many years and some, like Siringo's book, are still in print. But none of them tells much about the humdrum hard work that was the daily routine of ranching. Branding was one of the more exciting chores. Left, a calf is getting the hot iron. Right, a branding crew around the chuck wagon on the Matador Ranch about 1885.

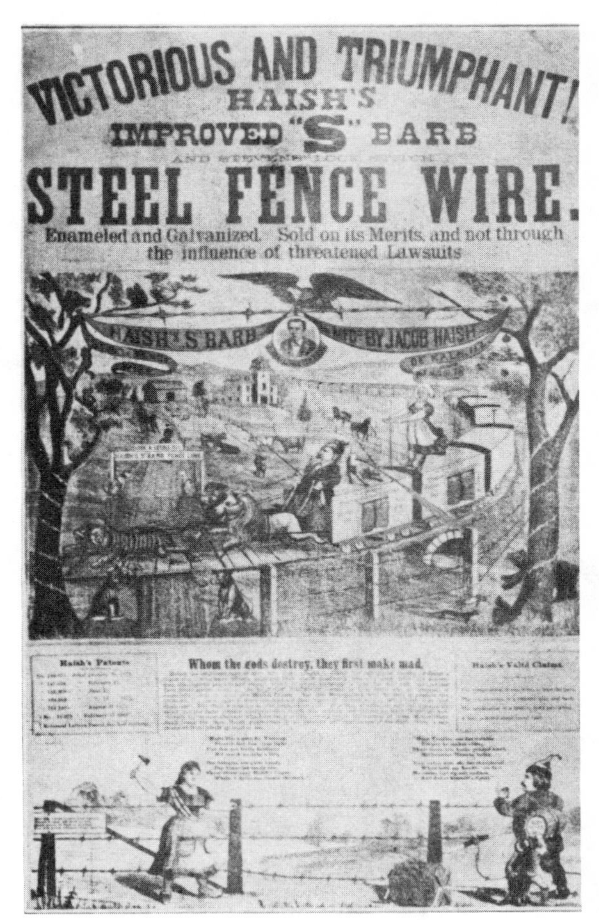

The windmill and barbed wire stimulated ranching and then helped kill it by making it possible and profitable to turn ranches into farms. Windmill shown here pumped water for cattle and later to irrigate crops. This wire manufacturer boasted he did not promote sales through threatened lawsuits. Weather was never good on the range—sand storms, heat, cold, rain—nothing in moderation.

The Discovery Well at Spindletop blows in.

CHAPTER 14

BLACK MAGIC

On the tenth day of the twentieth century Texas added a new and greater economic symbol to her cotton and her steers. That day the Spindletop gusher blew in near Beaumont to transform the economy of the region and usher in the modern petroleum era throughout the world. Derrick and refinery have overshadowed the cotton boll and the longhorn.

It began three hundred and thirty-eight years after De Soto's men found oil along the Texas coast not far from Spindletop. But neither they nor the Mexican nor the Anglo-American settlers guessed the value of the gummy, smelly oil seeps in East Texas; it remained for post-Civil War men to drill—unsuccessfully—for oil near Nacogdoches.

Spindletop field is still producing and experienced a second boom in 1925, when Yount-Lee brought in an 800-barrel gusher from 2,588 feet. But by then the field was controlled by three major companies and there was no such orgy of speculation as the 1901 boom caused.

The first real strike came in Central Texas, when the town of Corsicana drilled for water and hit oil. A few citizens believed what they had found was more valuable than water, and veterans from Pennsylvania—where oil had been produced since 1859—flocked to Corsicana and built a refinery that produced more kerosene for lamps than gasoline. Small quantities of oil were found in other parts of the state, but this late nineteenth-century oil flurry was only a curtain raiser for Spindletop.

Near Beaumont, a sleepy rice-market town of 10,000, Patillo Higgins had been drilling for oil for ten years. He was joined by A. F. Lucas, an Austrian-born engineer who had prospected for gold and salt and oil in various parts of the United States. When local capital was exhausted, he found backing in Pennsylvania and continued drilling at Spindletop.

On the morning of January 10, 1901, so the local paper reported, "an explosion occurred that forced the tubing into the air like a mere plaything, and then immediately followed a stream of black petroleum." The report added "the result will be highly beneficial to Beaumont," as indeed it was. In three months it was a city of 30,000, with $40 an acre land selling for $40,000, oil three cents a barrel, water five cents a cup.

J. F. Cotton found oil seepage in the Big Thicket of East Texas in 1859 and used it for a hog wallow. In 1865 he and a partner sank a well 100 feet, found evidence of gas and oil in what is now the Saratoga field, but lacked machinery to drill deeper. The well never produced but it still seeps oil.

The roar of Spindletop was heard around the world. Experienced oil men, speculators, all sorts of men flocked there to make and lose fortunes and flood the state and region with oil stock at ten cents a share. Within a year Beaumont oil was burning in Germany, England, Cuba, Mexico, New York, and Philadelphia. Texas ushered in the petroleum era for the whole world.

Total petroleum production in the United States aggregated only one billion barrels before 1901—the amount now produced annually by Texas wells. One of each seven barrels of the world's oil today is Texas oil, and one out of each eight Texans is employed in the industry.

From the Gulf coast drilling spread to all parts of the state—Petrolia, 1904; Electra, 1911; Ranger, 1917 (which furnished oil for World War I), Burkburnett, Breckenridge, and Desdemona in 1920, followed by Luling and Mexia. In every part of Texas during the twenties and thirties a forest of derricks sprang up.

Dad Joiner's Discovery Well in East Texas.

Discovery of oil at Breckenridge in 1920 brought another frenzy of speculation. More leases were bought and sold on curbstones than in offices.

In September, 1930, C. M. (Dad) Joiner, veteran wildcatter, proved the sensational East Texas field—about two hundred square miles with oil under every inch of it. It alone produced three billion barrels in less than a quarter of a century.

Strikes continued until Texas was producing during the single decade ending 1955 more than nine billion barrels—about as much as she had produced during the preceding half century. The value of her oil was about twice that of all her crops and livestock combined.

Only 50 of her 254 counties lack oil activity, and the acreage under lease for oil and gas exceeds the combined area of Massachusetts, Vermont, Rhode Island, Delaware, New Jersey, Maryland, West Virginia, and the District of Columbia.

The Kilgore Field includes the townsite.

Petroleum production has not only revolutionized Texas economy but has markedly changed the appearance of Texas. Derricks in fields in every part of the state, gas tank farms above *and refineries* right *enliven the Texas landscape.*

Along with oil production came gas distribution and a multitude of industrial enterprises that not only urbanized the state but made manufacturing only slightly less profitable than mineral extraction. And, like the cattle industry, petroleum has produced its folk heroes and its stereotyped personalities more often encountered in fiction than in the everyday life of the state.

CHAPTER 15

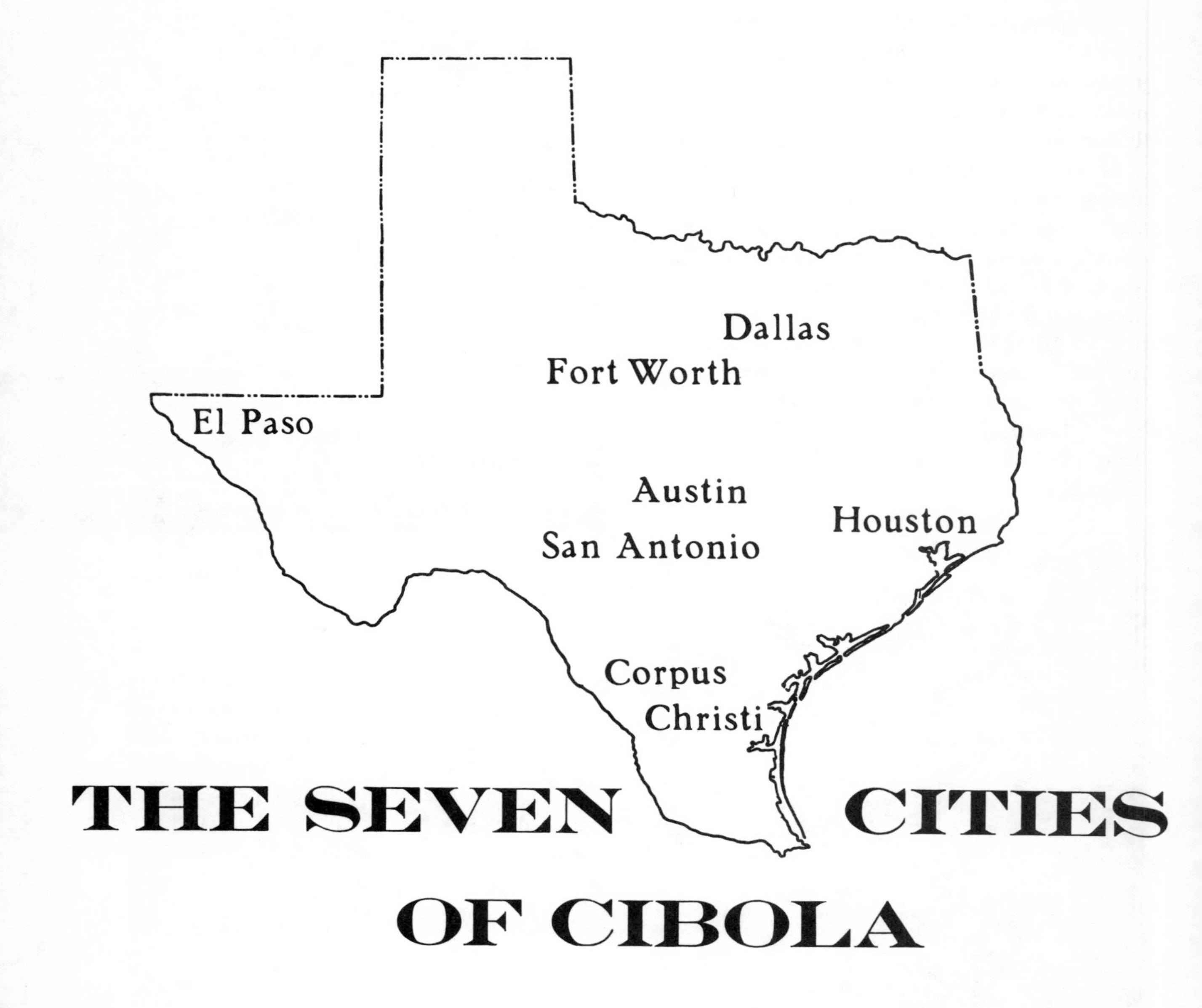

THE SEVEN CITIES OF CIBOLA

To find the Seven Cities of Cibola, white men first trekked across Texas four hundred years ago. They found none of them, neither in Texas nor elsewhere; for the riches of Cibola, like Cibola itself, were nothing more than myths. But if Coronado could return four centuries later he would find Seven Cities richer than those of Cibola were said to have been. Their riches are not in precious minerals and stones, but in people and commerce and manufacturing, and the institutions of culture.

In a general way the Seven Cities of Texas are very much alike. All are young and vigorous, still expanding, still aspiring. Although some of them stand on ancient foundations, as things are reckoned in Texas, all have attained urban status within the memory of men still living. And each city has a distinctive personality, partly a product of its regional environment and natural advantages but more especially the reflection of the composite character of the people who call it home.

AUSTIN

Austin, named for the Father of Texas, became the capital of the Republic of Texas in 1839, when it was on the western fringe of settlements. Its broad Congress Avenue, widest street in the state, leads from the Colorado River to the pink granite capitol, which was built in the 1880s at a cost of three million acres of land. There are many of the eleemosynary institutions, the University of Texas, and other private colleges, as well as headquarters of many business and professional organizations. Many of the older structures of native limestone still stand to remind visitors of the earlier days of this busy commercial, educational, governmental, and industrial center whose population has grown from zero in 1839 to 184,850 in 1960.

HOUSTON

First Texas city in size is Houston, planned in 1837 by optimistic real-estate promoters fifty miles from the coast on Buffalo Bayou and declared the temporary capital of the Republic of Texas before its broad streets were laid out. It was not a "government town" but a "commercial venture." Its prosperity did not depend on the meager government pay roll its promoters prophesied—accurately, as it turned out—that it would be "the future commercial emporium." To a great degree Houston has always had some of the flavor of the Old South—many of its Negroes are from Louisiana and cling to Creole dialect; but it early became a city in fact as well as in name. Its chamber of commerce was incorporated by the Texas Congress in 1840; it had the first theaters in Texas; and it grew rich not only from the surrounding countryside, but from shipping. It became a port in 1841; by 1876 it was receiv-

The shrewd New Yorkers who founded Houston visualized it as a port city, although it is not on the coast. With considerable exaggeration they promised in 1837 that "Vessels from New York and New Orleans can sail without obstacle to this place," but eventually that was true. Local enterprise and government aid have made Houston a major American port.

ing ocean-going steamships, and subsequent improvements of the ship channel have made it the busiest port of the South. Its shipping totaled 52,293,262 tons in 1956. It was from Houston, also, that Texas rail construction began in the 1840s until now eleven railroads come into Houston to meet the sea. Industry developed along with transportation, and then came oil. Houston, near the Gulf fields, became headquarters for all phases of the petroleum industry. Its people are cosmopolitan, its cultural institutions varied, and with a population of almost a million, its future appears unlimited.

John K. Allen, a 27-year-old Congressman from Nacogdoches, with his brother, A. C., a former professor of mathematics, founded Houston in 1837. Its good location and their high-powered promotion made it a boom town overnight.

Modern Houston is the result of bringing the sea to the city.

San Antonio in 1840.

Market Square in San Antonio, 1880.

San Antonio—army town, Mexican town, German town, town of infinite charm—dates from 1718 and was the political center of Spanish Texas. Much of the colonial charm lingers there, but it has kept pace with modern developments. Important as its commercial activities are, to Texans and visitors alike it is the cradle of Texas liberty, the site of the Alamo and the nearby missions, the ideal place to spend a week, a month, or the rest of one's life. San Antonio is said to have among its residents more retired military men than any other city; most of them earlier served at the various posts there. Its population in 1960 was 584,471. The annual Fiesta de San Jacinto is the carnival season. Its Menger Hotel celebrated its one hundredth anniversary in 1959.

SAN ANTONIO

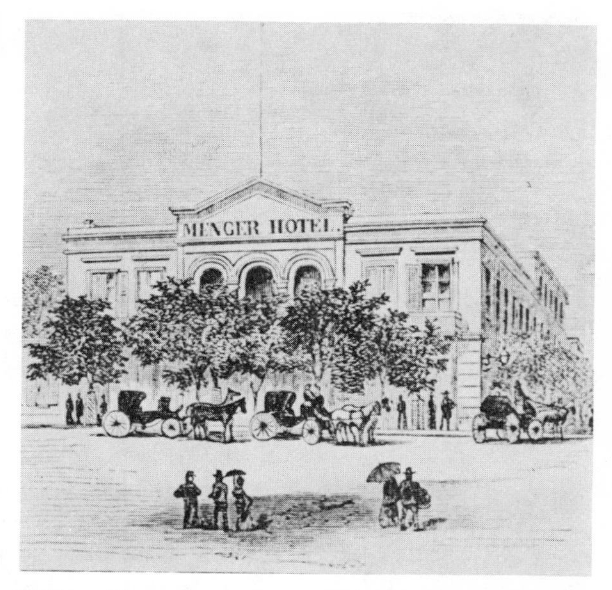

William Menger, a brewer, opened his hotel near his brewery on Alamo Plaza in 1859 and began enlarging it the next year. It became the best-known hotel in the southwest. It is the scene of several of O. Henry's stories, and its guest register contains such names as Sidney Lanier, Generals Sheridan, Belknap and Grant, and Theodore Roosevelt. Its famous bar, a replica of the taproom of the House of Lords Club, London, was a rendezvous for the Rough Riders in 1898. Modernization of the structure, which covers a block, has not destroyed its quaint charm.

Below. *A 20th century skyline and modern expressway give a new look to the City of the Alamo.*

Fort Worth was never a fort, but an army camp occupied the site from 1849 to 1853. It was named for General William J. Worth, U. S. A. When the soldiers moved away, citizens moved into the vacant buildings. The town was incorporated in 1873.

Fort Worth, site of an army camp 1849–53, grew slowly until the 1870s. It was a supply depot for cattlemen and after the railroad came in 1876 its stockyards were the largest in Texas. Packinghouses and flour mills followed and after 1915, when oil was struck in West Texas, it became an oil center. Population, 6,663 in 1880, has grown to over three hundred fifty thousand. Cow Town has become an urbane metropolitan city, as well known for its botanic gardens and cultural institutions as for its annual Fat Stock Show. During the decade of 1950s Fort Worth expanded toward the east and Dallas expanded westward until the thirty miles that separated their courthouses became a single urban district, containing a number of separately incorporated towns.

FT. WORTH

"Out Where the West Begins" has been a Fort Worth slogan for a century. The railroad ended there in 1876, and passengers proceeded via the Yuma stage line, which began operations in 1850. The distance, 1,600 miles, was covered in thirteen days. The daily arrival and departure of the Yuma stage was an exciting event in Fort Worth.

In the Spring Palace, Fort Worth displayed Texas resources until it burned in 1890.

CORPUS CHRISTI

Corpus Christi today bears little resemblance to H. L. Kinney's trading post of 1840 or Army Depot that was there 1845–55. It has been a port since 1854, and today is one of the 12 busiest in the nation. Its varied industries have made it a cosmopolitan, thriving, expanding city.

From a trading post guarded by a private army to a city of 150,000 in a century, that is the Corpus Christi story. A tent town sprang up in 1846 when General Taylor's army arrived. By 1860 it was a port as well as a post office and county seat. Wool, hides, cattle by-products, with shipping made it a town of about eight thousand by 1910, but it was oil production in 1916 and the creation of a deep-water port in 1926 that made it the fastest-growing city in Texas, and perhaps in the nation. Intercoastal and oceanic commerce, processing of petroleum and agricultural products, and varied industries brought a doubling of the population during the 1930s, and in 1960 more than 166,000 people lived there. It is a vacation resort with many attractions, including an annual Buccaneer Days Fiesta and a Writers' Conference. Its beautiful port facility was designed by sculptor Gutzon Borglum.

EL PASO

El Paso, the most western of Texas cities, stands at the Paso del Norte, through which Spanish explorers entered New Mexico in the sixteenth century. The modern city dates from the late 1840s, when cattle drives and forty-niners en route to California paused there; it was also a station on the Butterfield overland mail route; but the town site was not surveyed and the name El Paso chosen until about 1859. In 1877 Fort Bliss was established nearby, and by 1881 four railroads were put through the town. Until the turn of the century it was a "lead and likker town," famous for its gambling houses and vice resorts and killings; but after 1905 it took on a more civilized aspect. Like San Antonio, it is an army town and a vacation center, where the sunshine spends the winter. Lead smelting, milling, packing are among its industries. Its 1960 population was 271,903.

Four little settlements, the oldest dating from 1827, occupied the present site of El Paso, the name adopted in 1859. It was the scene of Confederate and Union activity during the Civil War, and permanent city government was delayed until 1880. Across the river is Ciudad Juárez.

Dallas didn't happen, it was created. Through the years its people have shaped its development to fit prevailing economic trends—if they could not control the trends. This earliest panorama of the city, for example, shows a train that wouldn't reach Dallas for another year. The view of courthouse square in 1879 shows the active cotton market. A few years later it was scene of the largest buffalo hide market in America. When the buffalo was gone, cowhides made Dallas the number-one leather market. When the automobile replaced the horse, automotive plants began to dot the industrial district; and as rail transportation declines, vast aeronautical and electronic enterprises are launched.

DALLAS

Dallas, first settled in 1841, has long been a financial, commercial, medical and cultural center. Before 1860 a number of European families who were added to the population gave the town the air of a city. Rapid growth came after 1873 when rail lines from south and east crossed at Dallas. It became the world's largest inland cotton market and for a time was the nation's biggest market for farm machinery and leather goods. Without water transportation and with few natural advantages, Dallas is essentially a man-made city. From the start many Midwesterners have been attracted there and it has long been a distributing center for national concerns. It is second only to Hartford in the number of insurance companies based there, and is the home of a Federal Reserve Bank. For nearly a century it has been a good show town. It has a summer-long program of musical comedies, a symphony orchestra and a Theatre Center designed by Frank Lloyd Wright. It is a favorite convention and vacation city, with a population of 672,029.

These surveyor's tools carved Dallas out of the wilderness in the 1840's.

THE TEXAS CENTENNIAL

During 1936 Texas celebrated the hundredth anniversary of her independence. Each of the 254 counties commemorated the event, but the eyes of the world focused on Dallas, scene of the gigantic and glamorous Centennial Exposition.

But Texans looked back, not just over that hundred years of independence, but over the rich panoply of the four centuries that made Texas and Texans what they are.

Against a background of the docile Indians who gave the state their name moved proud Spaniards bringing horse and cattle and white man's civilization. Then came French intruders to spur Spain to sink deep roots into the land by sending friars, soldiers and families to make it a vital salient of her far-flung empire for a hundred years and more. Next the Mexicans were masters of that land; it was they who invited Anglo-Americans to settle there and generously gave them the farms and ranches denied them in the United States. The Old Three Hundred and other colonists (they called themselves Texians) came from everywhere to create a new American frontier and transform it into a sovereign nation that attracted international attention for a decade, then voluntarily joined the American Union. Texians of the Republic were followed by generations of Texans who simultaneously profited from and helped develop modern America.

For all this is the heritage of Texas.

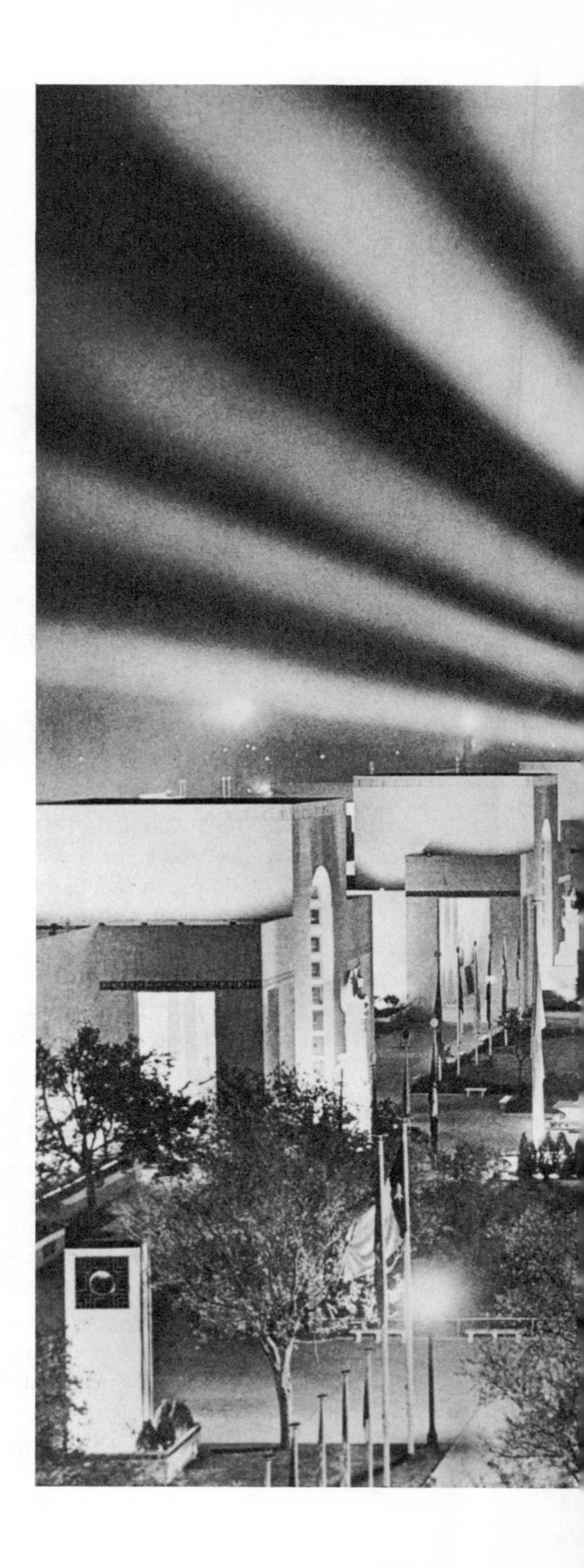

ACKNOWLEDGMENTS

The preparation of this pictorial history was an adventure in exploration—perhaps as exciting as and certainly more rewarding than Coronado's exploration of Texas.

The nuggets of gold which one discovers in depositories dedicated to preserving a record of Texas's past are exciting, even to one who knows in advance that the gold is there.

We are exceedingly grateful that the riches of many depositories have been graciously opened to us by those who have them in charge.

Mrs. David W. Knepper, director of the San Jacinto Museum of History, and her staff, were especially helpful in finding and reproducing rare materials in that institution which is so rich in pre-1860 Texana.

A. Garland Adair of the Texas Heritage Foundation made available pictures preserved through his indefatigable energy, which has recorded so much of Texas History.

DeWitt C. Greer, State Highway Engineer, furnished photographs from his department's excellent photographic collections.

W. C. Holden and Seymour V. Connor of Texas Technological College gave us access to the collections of the museum there.

Llerena Friend of the University of Texas aided us with materials in the Eugene C. Barker Texas History Center and with her own expert knowledge.

Dorman Winfrey, Texas State Archivist, helped us select priceless materials in the State Archives of the Texas State Library and arranged for their reproduction.

The Library of Congress, that major depository of everything American, and the New York Public Library, also yielded their Texas treasures.

We are grateful to have the privilege, through copyright permission and through artists' permission, to use some of the finest artistic recreations of the panorama of Texas. Certainly any Texas book is enriched by the works of Tom Lea, José Cisneros, and E. M. Schiwetz.

We were fortunate to have been situated in the midst of the valuable Texana collections of the Dallas Historical Society in the Hall of State. To all of the Society's staff, who have been as thoughtful and courteous as if we had been visiting scholars, and especially to Karl L. Gowin, whose expert advice on graphic presentation was most helpful, we are indebted for unfailing aid throughout the work.

A number of the photographs are from the splendid Hayes Collection, made available to the Dallas Historical Society by the Founders Group of the Dallas Garden Club.

Those who courteously gave permission to use copyrighted materials are listed on page 4. Non-copyrighted items are in the Texana collections of the Dallas Historical Society or in the personal collections of the authors, unless otherwise noted.

For the use of every item listed below we acknowledge our gratitude.

SOURCES OF ILLUSTRATIONS

Cattle Brands of Texas (end papers) are from the Officers' Dining Room of the First National Bank in Dallas. Courtesy First National Bank.

The Tejas Warrior (dust jacket), sculptured by Allie Tennant, stands above the central entrance of the Hall of State. Courtesy Dallas Historical Society.

Page

4. Hernando Cortes: Dallas Historical Society.
5. Cortes takes leave of the governor: Dallas Historical Society.
6. Pineda maps coast, by Frank Calder.
6. Cortes destroys idols: Dallas Historical Society.
7. First mass, Yucatan: Dallas Historical Society.

Page

8. Montezuma: San Jacinto Museum of History.
8. Ancient Mexico: San Jacinto Museum of History.
9. Grand Temple of Mexico: Library of Congress.
10. Aztec idols: San Jacinto Museum of History.
10. Mayan calendar: San Jacinto Museum of History.
11. Aztec sun god: San Jacinto Museum of History.
12. Cortes and Montezuma: Painting by Juan Ortega, San Carlos Academy of Fine Arts, Mexico City, courtesy American Embassy.
12. Cortes retakes Tenochtitlan, by Frank Calder.
13. Indian versions of the Spanish Conquest: *Natural History* (March, 1937), courtesy American Museum of Natural History.
14. Signature of Narváez: Dallas Historical Society.
15. DeVaca returns, by Tom Lea.
16. DeVaca heals sick, by E. M. Schiwetz.
17. DeVaca's coat of arms: courtesy Archivo de Indias, Seville.
18. DeVaca's book: New York Public Library.
19. DeSoto, by Reese Brandt.
22. Mendoza: Dallas Historical Society.
23. Soldier's armor: Dallas Historical Society.
24. Spanish buffalo drawing: Dallas Historical Society.
25. Coronado and the Turk: Etching by Norman Price, Dallas Historical Society.
26. Psalterium: University of Texas Library.
26. Our Lady of Guadalupe: San Jacinto Museum of History.
27. Chronicles of Franciscans: University of Texas Library.
28. Juan de Oñate, by Tom Lea.
30. Signature of Coronado: Dallas Historical Society.
31. Spanish priest and soldier, by Tom Lea.
33. Isleta Mission: Etching by Blanding Sloan, Dallas Historical Society.
34. Indians and LaSalle's ships, by E. M. Schiwetz.
35. LaSalle lands, by E. M. Schiwetz.
36. Spaniards with rattlesnake, pelican, buffalo and alligator, by E. M. Schiwetz.
39. Spanish sketch of Ft. St. Louis and markings on its door: University of Texas Library.
43. Baptismal fount: Dallas Historical Society.
43. Concepcion: San Jacinto Museum of History.
44-45. San José: Dallas Historical Society.
46. San Francisco de la Espada: University of Texas Library.
46. San Juan: Dallas Historical Society.
48. LaBahía: Dallas Historical Society.

Page

49. Report, 1783: Texas State Archives, Texas State Library.
50. Hidalgo: San Jacinto Museum of History.
51. Signatures, Hidalgo and Morelos: San Jacinto Museum of History.
51. Bean home: Dallas Historical Society.
52. Morelos and Calleja: San Jacinto Museum of History.
53. *Gaceta de Texas:* University of Texas Library.
55. Lafitte in battle, by Frank Calder.
56. Plan of Champ d'Asile: University of Texas Library.
57. Champ d'Asile: San Jacinto Museum of History.
63. Apodaca: Dallas Historical Society.
64. Governor's Palace stair: Dallas Historical Society.
64. Kitchen, Governor's Palace: Texas State Archives, Texas State Library.
65. Courtyard, Governor's Palace: Dallas Historical Society.
66. Iturbide: San Jacinto Museum of History.
66. Iturbide's coat of arms: San Jacinto Museum of History.
67. Juan O'Donojú: Dallas Historical Society.
68. Seal on Austin's passport: Texas Historical Survey Committee.
69. Stephen F. Austin: Painting, Texas State Capitol, courtesy A. Garland Adair, Texas Heritage Foundation.
70. Seals: Texas Historical Survey Committee.
71. Guadalupe Victoria, Extracto del plan, Mexican Federation, Mexican Constitution 1824: San Jacinto Museum of History.
72. Dress of Austin colonist: Drawing by Mary Reid of original costume, Dallas Historical Society.
73. Stephen F. Austin and Baron de Bastrop: Mural, Grand Central Station, Houston, Texas, by John McQuarrie.
74. Austin's homes at Peach Point and San Felipe; colony well: Dallas Historical Society.
77. Groce's Gin, by Frank Calder.
80. Old Stone Fort, by E. M. Schiwetz.
82. Frontiersman, by José Cisneros.
83. Fisher: Texas State Archives, Texas State Library.
85. Santa Anna: San Jacinto Museum of History.
86. Cos house: courtesy Texas Highway Department.
88. Petition: Dallas Historical Society.
89. Spanish halberd: San Jacinto Museum of History.
90. Broadside: San Jacinto Museum of History.

Page

91. Milam: Texas State Archives, Texas State Library.
91. Veramendi Palace: Library of Congress.
93. Commission: Texas State Archives, Texas State Library.
95. Travis letter: Texas State Archives, Texas State Library.
96. Crockett cartoon: San Jacinto Museum of History.
97. David Crockett: San Jacinto Museum of History.
99. Travis: Statue by Pompeo Coppini, Hall of State, Dallas Historical Society.
100. Washington-on-the-Brazos: Etching by Blanding Sloan, Dallas Historical Society.
101. Handbill: San Jacinto Museum of History.
102. Childress: Dallas Historical Society.
103. Texas Declaration of Independence: Texas State Archives, Texas State Library.
104. Fannin: Statue by Pompeo Coppini, Hall of State, Dallas Historical Society.
104. Fannin watch: Texas State Archives, Texas State Library.
105. Goliad: Etching by Norman Price, Dallas Historical Society.
106. Houston's March, by E. M. Schiwetz.
106. Deaf Smith: San Jacinto Museum of History.
107. Sam Houston: Painting by Seymour Thomas, San Jacinto Museum of History.
108. San Jacinto flag: Texas State Archives, Texas State Library, courtesy A. Garland Adair, Texas Heritage Foundation.
109. Santa Anna's flag: Dallas Historical Society.
109. Map, Battle of San Jacinto, by E. M. Schiwetz.
109. Santa Anna's spurs: Dallas Historical Society.
110-11. Battle of San Jacinto: Painting by H. A. McArdle, Texas State Capitol, courtesy A. Garland Adair, Texas Heritage Foundation.
112. Santa Anna before Houston: Painting by William H. Huddle, Texas State Capitol.
113. Sam Houston's report of the Battle of San Jacinto: Dallas Historical Society.
113. Magnolia leaves: Irion Collection.
114. San Jacinto Monument: San Jacinto Museum of History.
115. Currency: courtesy W. A. Philpott, Jr., editor, *Texas Bankers Record.*
117. Horse Marines and map of Gulf, by E. M. Schiwetz.
118. *"Mrs. Caroline Harris . . .",* Library of Congress.
119. Executive Mansion at Houston: Texas State Archives, Texas State Library.

Page

120. DeMorse House: Dallas Historical Society.
120. Blue and McIntyre houses: Library of Congress.
121. Freeman Inn: Dallas Historical Society.
121. Toalson and Chambers houses: Library of Congress.
123. Invitations: Dallas Historical Society.
123. McKinney dress: Drawing by Mary Reid.
123. Theater advertisement: Masonic Grand Lodge Library.
124. Broadside: Library of Congress.
125. British treaty: Texas State Archives, Texas State Library, courtesy A. Garland Adair, Texas Heritage Foundation.
126. Lamar: San Jacinto Museum of History.
129. Comanche: Dallas Historical Society.
131. Texas Legation Seal: Texas Historical Survey Committee.
131. French Embassy: courtesy Texas State Highway Department.
132. Texas Navy: San Jacinto Museum of History.
133. Texas Navy: Etching by Norman Price, Dallas Historical Society.
134. Anchor, by E. M. Schiwetz.
135. Polk and Dallas flag: Dallas Historical Society.
139. *True Blue:* Dallas Historical Society.
140. Capitol at Houston: San Jacinto Museum of History.
141. *Annexation a Case of War:* Library of Congress.
142. Schooner *San Antonio,* and map, by E. M. Schiwetz.
143. Sloop *Austin:* University of Texas Library.
146. Cartoon: Dallas Historical Society.
147. "Virtuous Harry": Dallas Historical Society.
147. Texas Demonstration: Library of Congress.
148. Jones House: Dallas Historical Society.
148. Capitol at Austin: University of Texas Library.
150. Great Seal: Texas State Archives, Texas State Library, courtesy A. Garland Adair, Texas Heritage Foundation.
152. Army of Occupation: Library of Congress.
153. Battle and plan of Palo Alto: Library of Congress.
154. Gun: University of Texas Library.
155. Our army and Battle of Buena Vista: University of Texas Library.
156-57. Chamberlain drawings: San Jacinto Museum of History.
158. Texian Campaigne china: Texas State Archives, Texas State Library.
159. Running the line: San Jacinto Museum of History.

Page

160. Governors Wood and Bell: Paintings Texas State Capitol, courtesy A. Garland Adair, Texas Heritage Foundation.
161. Governor's Mansion: courtesy Austin Chamber of Commerce.
162-63. Fort Brown, Fort Clark, Fort Ringgold, cannon, Fort McIntosh, by E. M. Schiwetz.
164. Wyalucing: Dallas Historical Society.
164. Cartwright House: Dallas Historical Society.
165. Pease mansion: Dallas Historical Society.
166. Solms-Braunfels: courtesy Oscar Haas.
166. Indianola: University of Texas Library.
167. Marshall: Texas State Archives, Texas State Library.
167. Fredericksburg: Dallas Historical Society.
169. Seal of Confederacy: Dallas Historical Society.
170. Joint resolution: Library of Congress.
171. General Twigg and his surrender: Dallas Historical Society.
172. Bivouac of Confederate troops: Dallas Historical Society.
173. Attack on gunboats and attack at Galveston: Dallas Historical Society.
174. General J. B. MacGruder: Dallas Historical Society.
175. Panorama of war: Library of Congress.
175. Attack on Sabine Pass: Dallas Historical Society.
176. Evacuating Brownsville: Dallas Historical Society.
177. Texas Ranger: Dallas Historical Society.
177. John H. Roberts and Benjamin Roberts: courtesy Summerfield G. Roberts.
178. John S. Ford, by Tom Lea.
179. Train: by José Cisneros.
180. Governor Throckmorton: Painting, Texas State Capitol, courtesy A. Garland Adair, Texas Heritage Foundation.
180. Throckmorton and Pease correspondence: Dallas Historical Society.
181. Immigrants: Dallas Historical Society.
183. Branding iron: Dallas Historical Society.
184. Buffalo hunters' camp and Texas hunters: Dallas Historical Society.
185. Spaniards bring cattle: Painting by Tom Lea, courtesy Dallas Museum of Fine Arts.
186. Texas longhorn: Painting by Tom Lea, courtesy Dallas Museum of Fine Arts.
187. Where the bronco twister gets his name, by Will James: The Thomas Gilcrease Institute of American History and Art.
188. Chucktime on the Lazy R: Painting by Harry Anthony de Young, Anacacho Room, St. Anthony Hotel, San Antonio, courtesy of the Directors of the St. Anthony.
192. *Comanche Dick:* Library of Congress.
192. Branding, Mosier Ranch: courtesy Texas State Highway Department.
192. *A Texas Cowboy:* Library of Congress.
192. Matador branding outfit, 1885: Texas Technological College.
193. Barbwire: courtesy American Steel and Wire Division of United States Steel Corporation.
193. Wet morning on the Circle O: Painting by Olaf Seltzer, The Thomas Gilcrease Institute of American History and Art.
194. Spindletop discovery well: Dallas Historical Society.
195. Spindletop field: Dallas Historical Society.
196. Oldest existing Texas well, Saratoga: courtesy Texas Highway Department.
196. Joiner discovery well: Dallas Historical Society.
196. Curbstone oil stock brokers: University of Texas Library.
197. Kilgore, Texas, and Warringas tank farm: courtesy Texas Highway Department.
197. Humble Refinery at Overton: Dallas Historical Society.
199. Austin: courtesy Austin Chamber of Commerce.
200. Houston Ship Channel: courtesy Houston Chamber of Commerce.
200. Texas head of navigation: San Jacinto Museum of History.
201. John Kirby Allen: San Jacinto Museum of History.
201. Houston: courtesy Houston Lighting and Power Company.
202. San Antonio in 1880: Texas State Archives, Texas State Library.
203. Menger Hotel: Dallas Historical Society.
203. San Antonio: courtesy San Antonio Chamber of Commerce.
204. Camp Worth and Ft. Worth skyline: courtesy Ft. Worth Chamber of Commerce.
205. Yuma stage, Ft. Worth, and burning of Spring Palace: Dallas Historical Society.
206. Corpus Christi and industrial district: courtesy Corpus Christi Chamber of Commerce.
207. El Paso in 1868: Texas State Archives, Texas State Library.
207. El Paso: courtesy El Paso Chamber of Commerce.
208. Dallas in 1872 and 1879: Dallas Historical Society.
209. Surveying tools, Dallas: Dallas Historical Society.

INDEX